Family in the Bible

Family in the Bible

Exploring Customs, Culture, and Context

edited by
Richard S. Hess and
M. Daniel Carroll R.

 Baker Academic

A Division of Baker Book House Co
Grand Rapids, Michigan 49516

©2003 by Richard S. Hess and M. Daniel Carroll R.

Published by Baker Academic
a division of Baker Book House Company
P.O. Box 6287, Grand Rapids, MI 49516-6287
www.bakeracademic.com

Printed in the United States of America

Library of Congress Cataloging-in-Publication Data
Family in the Bible : exploring customs, culture, and context / edited by
  Richard S. Hess and M. Daniel Carroll R.
       p.   cm.
    Includes bibliographical references and indexes.
    ISBN 0-8010-2628-8 (pbk.)
    1. Family—Biblical teaching. I. Hess, Richard S. II. Carroll R., M.
  Daniel.
  BS680.F3F36 2003
  220.8′30685—dc21   2003051882

Contents

List of Contributors   7
Editors' Preface   8
List of Abbreviations   11

Part 1: Family in the Old Testament
1. Family in the Pentateuch   17
   —*Gordon J. Wenham*
2. Family in the Non-narrative Sections
   of the Pentateuch   32
   —*Edesio Sánchez*
3. Family in the Historical Books   59
   —*David T. Tsumura*
4. Family in the Wisdom Literature   80
   —*Tremper Longman III*
5. Family in the Prophetic Literature   100
   —*M. Daniel Carroll R.*

Part 2: Family in the New Testament
6. Family in the Gospels and Acts   125
   —*Cynthia Long Westfall*
7. Family in the Epistles   148
   —*Stanley E. Porter*

Index of Scripture and Other Ancient Writings   167
Index of Modern Authors   173

107840

Contributors

M. Daniel Carroll R. (Rodas), Ph.D.
Professor of Old Testament
Denver Seminary, Denver, Colorado
Adjunct Professor
El Seminario Teológico Centroamericano, Guatemala City, Guatemala

Tremper Longman III, Ph.D.
Professor of Old Testament
Westmont College, Santa Barbara, California

Stanley E. Porter, Ph.D.
Principal, Dean, and Professor of New Testament
McMaster Divinity College, McMaster University, Hamilton, Canada

Edesio Sánchez, Ph.D.
Translation Consultant for United Bible Societies
San José, Costa Rica

David T. Tsumura, Ph.D.
Professor of Old Testament
Japan Bible Seminary, Tokyo, Japan

Gordon J. Wenham, Ph.D.
Professor of Old Testament
University of Gloucestershire, Cheltenham, England

Cynthia Long Westfall, Ph.D.
Adjunct Professor in Biblical Studies
Colorado Christian University, Denver, Colorado

Editors' Preface

We are delighted to see this volume completed and made available. It contains papers presented at the third annual biblical studies conference of the Denver Institute for Contextualized Biblical Studies of Denver Seminary, held February 1–2, 2002, as well as several that were commissioned especially for this publication.[1]

Family in the Bible provides one of the few studies of the family that surveys its appearance throughout the entire Bible. Although all of the contributors represent an evangelical view of the Bible and its value for addressing the Christian faith in practical ways, this book is not a collection of biblical commands that unthinkingly or simplistically applies ancient models of behavior to modern lifestyles. Far from that, it represents an attempt to appreciate the role of the family as the central element of society in the biblical worldview. As such, the customs and life of the family are evaluated in light of the surrounding cultures and in their overall context in the pages of the Old and New Testaments. The result is a picture of family life that extends well beyond preconceived ideas and looks at the diversity of lives contained within the Bible.

The choice of contributors includes the leading scholars in their specialties of biblical studies in order to obtain a view that is conversant with the latest developments in scholarship. From the beginning, this collection also was designed to reflect

1. The papers from the second annual conference appear in Richard S. Hess and M. Daniel Carroll R., eds., *Israel's Messiah in the Bible and the Dead Sea Scrolls* (Grand Rapids: Baker, 2003).

a high degree of balance and continuity through the various major sections of the literature of the Bible. Finally, as has been the practice in every conference of the Institute, the contributors were selected to represent evangelical scholarship from a breadth of theological persuasions, institutions, and nationalities in order to foster serious research and constructive dialogue among those who are committed to making the Bible come alive for today's world.

Professor Wenham, a British scholar known for his important work in Genesis, sets the stage for the rest of the volume with a sweep of the foundational narratives of that first book of the Bible and beyond. He places these accounts within the very different cultural context of the patriarchs before suggesting constructive insights for modern family life. Dr. Sánchez, a Latin American who works in Costa Rica, reviews the legal material in the Pentateuch, in particular the Book of Deuteronomy, with the goal of establishing the centrality of the home for nurturing faith in God. Japanese scholar Professor Tsumura contributes a chapter of both erudition and clarity in his study of the family in the historical books. He surveys a number of challenges faced by families in ancient Israel and offers a wealth of examples gleaned from this material to illustrate his presentation. Professor Longman brings his expertise to the study of the Wisdom and poetic literature. His focus is primarily on the Book of Proverbs, in which he finds multiple lessons for the husband-wife relationship and the raising of children who would fear God. Professor Carroll R. completes this discussion of the family in the Old Testament with an examination of prophetic texts. Controversy surrounds this vast collection of literature, both for its original audience and for the modern interpreter, yet these books have much to teach us about divine expectations for the family in worship and ethical practice and are a rich source of familial metaphors for Yahweh and his relationship with his people.

The final two essays address the New Testament. Professor Westfall makes an important contribution that demonstrates how Jesus both strengthened and challenged family life in first-century Palestine. Her work is also a very creative piece that examines Jesus' own family experience, which resulted from the circumstances of his birth and the realities of his unique person and calling. From Canada, Professor Porter concludes our collection with a careful analysis of the various kinds of lexical data for the family in the Epistles. His work demonstrates how, despite the virtual absence of the specific term "family," concepts grounded in several dimensions of family life of that time played a critical role in defining the Christian's position in the family of God and enabled so many alienated persons of the first century to find hope and salvation in that family.

As editors, our commitment has been to give the contributors maximum freedom, without demanding agreement on every issue. We believe that this has resulted in a useful and timely discussion of the family in the Bible that can be of much profit to every scholar, pastor, and teacher in both the academic and the pastoral arenas.

Richard S. Hess
M. Daniel Carroll R.
All Saints' Day
November 1, 2002

Abbreviations

AB   Anchor Bible

ABD   *Anchor Bible Dictionary*, ed. D. N. Freedman, 6 vols. (New York: Doubleday, 1992)

ABR   *Australian Biblical Review*

ABRL   Anchor Bible Reference Library

AOAT   Alter Orient und Altes Testament

AUSS   *Andrews University Seminary Studies*

BASOR   *Bulletin of the American Schools of Oriental Research*

BDAG   W. Bauer, F. W. Danker, W. F. Arndt, and F. W. Gingrich, *A Greek-English Lexicon of the New Testament and Other Early Christian Literature,* 3d ed. (Chicago: University of Chicago Press, 2000)

CAD   *The Assyrian Dictionary of the Oriental Institute of the University of Chicago*, ed. I. J. Gelb et al. (Chicago: Oriental Institute, 1956–)

CBQ   *Catholic Biblical Quarterly*

CTA   *Corpus des tablettes en cunéiformes alphabétiques découvertes à Ras Shamra-Ugarit de 1929 à 1939*, ed. A. Herdner, Mission de Ras Shamra 10 (Paris: Imprimerie nationale, 1963)

DDD   *Dictionary of Deities and Demons in the Bible*, ed. K. van der Toorn, B. Becking, and P. W. van der Horst, rev. ed. (Leiden: Brill; Grand Rapids: Eerdmans, 1999)

DNTB   *Dictionary of New Testament Background*, ed. C. A. Evans and S. E. Porter (Downers Grove, Ill.: InterVarsity, 2000)

FN   *Filología neotestamentaria*

FOTL   Forms of Old Testament Literature

GTJ   *Grace Theological Journal*

HALOT   L. Koehler, W. Baumgartner, and J. J. Stamm, *The Hebrew and Aramaic Lexicon of the Old Testament,* trans. and ed. M. E. J. Richardson, 4 vols. (Leiden: Brill, 1994–99)

HeyJ   *Heythrop Journal*

HS   *Hebrew Studies*

HSM   Harvard Semitic Monographs

HTKNT   Herders theologischer Kommentar zum Neuen Testament

HUCA   *Hebrew Union College Annual*

ICC   International Critical Commentary

IDB   *Interpreter's Dictionary of the Bible,* ed. G. A. Buttrick, 4 vols. (Nashville: Abingdon, 1962)

Int   *Interpretation*

JBL   *Journal of Biblical Literature*

JPsychTh   *Journal of Psychology and Theology*

JSNT   *Journal for the Study of the New Testament*

JSNTSup   Journal for the Study of the New Testament: Supplement Series

JSOT   *Journal for the Study of the Old Testament*

JSOTSup   Journal for the Study of the Old Testament: Supplement Series

KTU   *Die keilalphabetischen Texte aus Ugarit,* ed. M. Dietrich, O. Loretz, and J. Sanmartín, AOAT 24.1 (Kevelaer: Butzon & Berker; Neukirchen-Vluyn: Neukirchener Verlag, 1976)

MT   Masoretic Text

NAC   New American Commentary

NCB   New Century Bible

NICNT   New International Commentary on the New Testament

NICOT   New International Commentary on the Old Testament

NIDOTTE   *New International Dictionary of Old Testament Theology and Exegesis,* ed. W. A. VanGemeren, 5 vols. (Grand Rapids: Zondervan, 1997)

NIV   New International Version

NJPS   *Tanakh: The Holy Scriptures: The New Jewish Publication Society Translation according to the Traditional Hebrew Text*

NLT   New Living Translation

NRSV   New Revised Standard Version

NSBT   New Studies in Biblical Theology

OBT   Overtures to Biblical Theology

OTL   Old Testament Library

RB   *Revue biblique*

SAHL   Studies in the Archaeology and History of the Levant

SBG   Studies in Biblical Greek

SBLDS   Society of Biblical Literature Dissertation Series

SBLMS   Society of Biblical Literature Monograph Series

SBLSBS   Society of Biblical Literature Sources for Biblical Study

SJT   *Scottish Journal of Theology*

SP   Sacra Pagina

TEV   Today's English Version (Good News Bible)

TOTC   Tyndale Old Testament Commentaries

UF   *Ugarit-Forschungen*

UT   *Ugaritic Textbook*, ed. C. H. Gordon, Analecta orientalia 38
         (Rome: Pontifical Biblical Institute, 1965)

VTSup   Vetus Testamentum Supplements

WBC   Word Biblical Commentary

WTJ   *Westminster Theological Journal*

WUNT   Wissenschaftliche Untersuchungen zum Neuen Testament

PART 1

Family in the Old Testament

1

Family in the Pentateuch

GORDON J. WENHAM

"God settles the solitary in a home" (Ps. 68:6) expresses the Old Testament's positive view of community life. Genesis 2:18 puts it differently: "It is not good that the man should be alone" (NRSV). It then goes on to tell of God creating Eve for Adam to cure his loneliness. The stories of Genesis with their focus on family life are some of the best known in the Bible. Scholars debate the historicity of these tales, but the average Bible reader is simply impressed by their vividness and their faithful depiction of family life in so many situations that we can still identify with.

But in their very familiarity lurks danger. We in the West live in a world that is culturally quite different from theirs, and, unwittingly, as we read these stories to ourselves or retell them to our children, we may read into them customs and a worldview that are quite different from theirs. So, though we think that we may be understanding them, we are in fact profoundly misinterpreting them.

Some years ago a book by Walter Trobisch on marriage was published, entitled *I Married You*.[1] It contained much practical advice for young people intending to marry and was based on

1. Walter Trobisch, *I Married You* (New York: Harper & Row, 1971).

biblical principles and long experience of life in England and in
Nigeria. Quite rightly, the author discussed one of the key texts
on marriage in the Bible, Gen. 2:24: "Therefore a man shall
leave his father and mother and hold fast to his wife, and they
shall become one flesh." Trobisch went on to relate how he used
to expound this text to the Nigerians, telling them that it justi-
fies the Western practice of newly wed couples setting up home
on their own, well out of range of parental interference. In Nigeria, however, it was customary for the newlyweds to live in or
near the home of the husband's family. This, declared Trobisch,
was most undesirable for the new couple's relationship and was
condemned by this text from Genesis.

Unfortunately for his Nigerian listeners, Trobisch could not
have been more wrong, for the practice in Old Testament times
was much closer to Nigerian than to Western practice. The Israelites practiced patrilocal marriage: the man stayed near his
parents, for in due time he would inherit their land, and the
bride left her family to join her husband's extended family. So
why does Genesis speak of the man leaving his parents and
holding fast to his wife? Would it not be more accurate to say,
"Therefore a woman leaves her parents and holds fast to her
husband"?

What Trobisch, and doubtless many other Western readers,
failed to grasp about Gen. 2:24 was that "leave" was not meant
so much literally as emotionally. In traditional societies, the
most important social obligation is to one's parents. "Honor
your father and mother" is the first of the commands in the Decalogue regarding obligations to other people. But Genesis is saying that when a man marries, his order of responsibilities
changes: though his parents' needs are still important, his
wife's needs are even more important. Responsibility for her
welfare now must take priority even over care for his parents.

This profound insight about marriage is, of course, expounded even more clearly by Paul in Eph. 5, where he compares a man's love for his wife with Christ's love for the church.
Unfortunately, our missionary to Nigeria had missed this point
and tried to impose Western marriage patterns in a traditional
culture. But that is a minor point; my major concern is that we
are all liable to misinterpret the Old Testament stories about
family life if we read them as modern Westerners rather than

as Easterners of the second millennium B.C.E. We must shed our modern preconceptions and seek to recover the assumptions and outlook of the ancient world. This is no easy task, and even the most learned scholar would admit to being able to do it only imperfectly. However hard we try to escape our modern environment and understand the past from its own perspectives, we are limited in what we can achieve.

However, we can reduce the scale of our potential misunderstanding if we become more historically and sociologically self-conscious—that is, if we recognize the general difference between our society and theirs. We must acknowledge where we are coming from and where they were coming from. We must try to understand some of the fundamental structures of their society before we read the family stories contained in Genesis, for it is within those structures that they were heard in biblical times. For example, people knew what normally happened when someone married, had a child, or died in Israel, so when they heard a story about what one of their ancestors did in those circumstances, they would automatically compare the customs they knew with what the patriarchs did. We should try to do the same.

Furthermore, we need to recognize that not everything described in the narratives was understood to be normative. Believing readers of the Old Testament, whether Christian or Jewish, have always believed that "whatever was written in former days was written for our instruction" (Rom. 15:4 NRSV). But this is not to say that everything the patriarchs did in Genesis is supposed to be imitated. Sometimes they made big mistakes, which are recorded to encourage later readers to learn from them. But once again we need to be cautious lest we allow our instincts about what is right or wrong to be imposed on the text rather than let the biblical writers instruct us. We need to read the texts sensitively to discover what they are saying about the events described, not simply to let our gut reactions determine their significance for us.

In the rest of this essay I do five things. First, I sketch some of the biggest differences between biblical society and our own in the sphere of family life. Second, I outline some of the customs and practices associated with family that are alluded to in the Old Testament. Third, I look at the problem of disentangling historical descriptions of family life contained in Genesis from the author's ethical evaluation of these activities: how do we know when he is applauding the acts he describes and when he is criticizing them? Fourth, after discussing the ethics of the implied author, I ask what message about family life emerges from the stories of Genesis. Fifth, I ask what attitude we should take toward the structures of family life disclosed in the Bible: how far should Bible-believing Christians aim to resurrect institutions of biblical times, such as arranged marriages and patriarchy? Are these structures normative, paradigmatic, or illustrative?

Differences between Ancient Israelite and Modern Society

We begin with some broad-brush distinctions between the days of Genesis and our own. Obviously, they were technologically quite different from the developed Western world. No cell phones, television, electricity, motor vehicles, aircraft, hospitals, supermarkets, and so on. But more important from the point of view of this essay is their different view of the relationship between the individual and society. We live in a society in which everyone is supposed to be equal, independent, and free to choose his or her own way of life. Self-fulfillment and self-satisfaction are the great goals of our consumerist society.[2] Society is pictured as a collection of free-floating individuals, like molecules in a gas jar, impacting each other from time to time but with no permanent attachments to any other. Democracy, the will of the majority expressed through ballot box or opinion poll, determines what is right or wrong.

Biblical assumptions about society and the individual are quite different. You were who you were because of the family you were born into. Your family determined your career (e.g., farmer, priest, king), your land holding, where you lived, and where you died. Hence your genealogy was all-important and

2. For a discussion of these contrasts, see C. G. Bartholomew and T. Moritz, *Christ and Consumerism: Critical Reflections on the Spirit of Our Age* (Carlisle, U.K.: Paternoster, 2000).

enormously interesting, though for us genealogies seem to be the most boring parts of Scripture. You saw yourself not as a free-floating individual, but as part of a father's house, a clan, a tribe, a people. Israel, the nation, was one giant firm or company in which every member had a specific place and had a particular role to play. Every Israelite saw himself or herself as a member of a firm or team, or, more precisely, a variety of teams. The most significant team was your immediate extended family, but it in turn belonged to the larger teams such as the clan and the tribe. The individual's welfare depended on the success of the team to which he or she belonged. If a family's crops failed, its members might find themselves sold into slavery and their land mortgaged until the year of Jubilee. Thus, every individual saw his or her responsibility primarily to family or clan or tribe, not to self. And whereas modern individuals choose to work for a particular company or play in a particular team, in ancient Israel no male had much choice. You were born into a specific family in a particular place, and that determined your life thereafter.[3] Finally, democracy would have had little place in ancient thought. As far as day-to-day decisions were concerned, nearly everyone was answerable to someone higher up in the social structure, and at the top the king was answerable to God.

Patriarchal Family Life

These principles can be illustrated from the processes of family decision-making. Archaeologists have discovered that the earliest Israelite settlements consisted of small hamlets, with 50 to 150 people dwelling on an acre or two. The houses in such villages had three or four rooms on the ground floor, probably used for agricultural purposes such as storing grain or housing animals, and other rooms on the second floor presum-

3. Ironically, modern society, which prizes individual freedom and self-sufficiency so much, is in many ways more interdependent than ancient society. The ancients grew their own food on their own land and drew water from their local well. We are dependent on utilities for fuel and water and on supermarkets bringing food from places hundreds, if not thousands, of miles from where we live.

ably for human habitation. The houses themselves were built in groups of two or three around a common courtyard. Archaeologists surmise that a nuclear family lived in each house and that the houses sharing a common courtyard represented other nuclear families in the extended family, called the "father's house" in Hebrew.[4]

Unfortunately, archaeological evidence does not take us back any earlier than the judges period in Israel, but it is not difficult to imagine that the Israelites in Goshen in Egypt arranged themselves similarly. It is also possible that the patriarchs arranged their tents in this fashion. One certainly gets the impression from Genesis that Jacob lived near Laban, as he worked his fourteen years to earn the hand of Rachel and of Leah. When Jacob's sons were going to and fro between Canaan and Egypt, it is evident that the sons' wives and children were living close to grandfather Jacob. And although Jacob was too elderly to go down to Egypt to fetch grain, he had the ultimate authority over his sons: they went to buy grain only when he consented (Gen. 42:1–2; 43:1–2). Normally, when a man married, it was his wife who moved and became part of her husband's family, but Jacob continued living with his uncle and father-in-law, Laban. This meant that Jacob had to submit to Laban's demand that he stay and work for him. It was only by tricking Laban that Jacob eventually escaped his control (see Gen. 31). Within the nuclear family, children were expected to obey their parents, and wives were subject to their husbands. This is illustrated by the laws on vows in Num. 30. If a man makes a vow, he must carry it out. However, if a woman makes a vow, her father (if she is a minor) or her husband (if she is married) may veto the vow; in that case, she is no longer obliged to fulfill it.

But this is not to say that women did not have a significant say in family decision-making processes. Numbers 30 indicates that they could initiate vows themselves. Meyers points out that women were very important workers in the household and probably were responsible for many of the skilled tasks in pro-

4. Carol Meyers, "The Family in Early Israel," in *Families in Ancient Israel*, ed. L. G. Perdue et al., The Family, Religion, and Culture (Louisville: Westminster John Knox, 1997), 12–19; Amihai Mazar, *Archaeology of the Land of the Bible, 10,000—586 B.C.E.*, ABRL (New York: Doubleday, 1992), 338–45, 485–89.

cessing farm products, such as spinning, weaving, grinding grain, and cooking, as well as bearing and training children. This would have given them considerable authority within the household.[5] Certainly the "excellent wife" of Prov. 31 and Rebekah in Genesis are portrayed as women with great energy and initiative, dedicated to the well-being of their households.

Marriage customs also illustrate the authority structures within Israelite families. Isaac and Jacob found their wives in very different ways. In the case of Isaac and Rebekah, neither saw the other before the match was agreed upon. Abraham's servant went to the city of Nahor and met Rebekah by the well. He negotiated marriage terms with her father and brother, and she consented to leave promptly. That this totally arranged marriage was divinely organized is heavily underlined by the participants in the story and by the narrator (e.g., Gen. 24:50–51). On the other hand, Jacob and Esau take the initiative themselves. Isaac and Rebekah did not like Esau's choice, so they sent Jacob to find a wife from their relatives, which he did. But because he had no parental backup to manage his wedding arrangements, he was badly cheated by his father-in-law. It seems likely that the experiences of Isaac and Jacob were extreme cases of total parental control, on the one hand, and no control at all, on the other. Perhaps Samson's case was more typical: he noticed a girl whom he fancied and told his father and mother, "Get her for me as my wife" (Judg. 14:2 NRSV).

Though the case of Jacob and Rachel shows that it was possible to find a wife without parental involvement, it was more difficult to proceed to betrothal, for this involved a large capital transfer from the man's family to the woman's family. The marriage payment, or bride price (*mōhar*), typically was equivalent to several years' wages.[6] Since he could not e-mail home for credit, Jacob had to work for his father-in-law for seven years before he could marry Rachel. When the wedding came, the couple still were dependent on their parents, first to provide the

5. Meyers, "Family in Early Isarel," 32–37.
6. In Old Babylonian contracts the marriage present ranged from one to forty shekels (see G. R. Driver and J. C. Miles, *The Babylonian Laws* [Oxford: Clarendon, 1952], 1:250 n. 4), and a shepherd's annual wage was six shekels (ibid., 1:471). The maximum marriage present allowed by Deut. 22:29 is fifty shekels.

seven-day-long wedding feast (Gen. 29:22–29; cf. Judg. 14:12) and for payment of the dowry. The dowry was the large wedding present given by the bride's father to her on her wedding day. Typically it consisted of furniture, clothing, and money, but in the case of Rachel and Leah, it also contained slave girls. The dowry remained the property of the bride throughout her marriage and had to be preserved intact by her husband, so that if he died or divorced her, she had something to fall back on.[7]

Description and Evaluation of Patriarchal Life

These brief comments about some key features of family life in the Pentateuch are a necessary preliminary to the central interpretative issue: How do we discern the author's standpoint on the events he relates? If we do not answer this question correctly, we are liable to misuse the Bible totally, taking stories written to warn of the dangers of certain behavior as examples to imitate and vice versa. Does the writer of Genesis commend Abraham's attempt to disguise the status of Sarah as his wife, or Jacob's deceit of his father, Isaac? Some famous scholars have held that the author does approve of these actions. Whose side is the author on when he tells the story of Dinah's rape and the subsequent massacre in the city of Shechem?

These are difficult questions to answer, and I return to them frequently in my commentary on Genesis. More recently, I have devoted a book to the issue, *Story as Torah*.[8] Here I can only sketch the argument and summarize some of the conclusions.

In reading the lives of the patriarchs, we cannot discover the author's standpoint simply by looking at these stories in isolation, for he gives too few clues as to what he thinks about the actors' behavior. Express moralizing comments are rare in Genesis, as in the rest of the Bible. In the context of the whole

7. For further discussion of biblical marriage customs, see M. Burrows, *The Basis of Israelite Marriage* (New Haven: American Oriental Society, 1938); and G. P. Hugenberger, *Marriage as a Covenant: Biblical Law and Ethics as Developed from Malachi*, VTSup 52 (Leiden: Brill, 1994; reprint, Grand Rapids: Baker, 1998).

8. Gordon J. Wenham, *Story as Torah: Reading the Old Testament Ethically*, Old Testament Studies (Edinburgh: Clark, 2000), esp. chs. 5 and 6.

book, however, he does disclose his hand sufficiently for us to come to some quite firm conclusions.

"Information and attitudes presented at an early stage of the text tend to encourage the reader to interpret everything in their light,"[9] states literary critic Rimmon-Kenan. This suggests that the opening chapters of Genesis may well give some clear clues about the writer's convictions. Chapters 1 and 2 tell of the world that God designed before sin disrupted everything. They paint a picture of a world at harmony, which contrasts vividly with the dissension that characterizes the human story from chapter 3 onward. In so doing, they drop hints about what family life should be like.

The first command given to humankind is "Be fruitful and multiply and fill the earth and subdue it" (Gen. 1:28 NRSV). This foreshadows the promises made to the patriarchs, such as "I will make of you a great nation" (12:2 NRSV) and "I will make your offspring like the dust of the earth, so that if one can count the dust of the earth, your offspring also can be counted" (13:16 NRSV). Children, in other words, are viewed very positively. There is no fear of a population explosion, such as we find in the Atrahasis Epic from the second millennium B.C.E. or in some modern demographers. The desire for children is so strong that Rachel screams at Jacob, "Give me children, or I shall die!" (30:1 NRSV). Sarah's and Rebekah's long periods of childlessness are poignant, not simply because ancient Israelite women longed to be mothers but also because they had been promised children by God. Children were seen as the family's most precious possession; so God's demand to Abraham to offer his only son must have pained him beyond words, while Lot's rash readiness to sacrifice his daughters to the Sodom mob shows his desperation to protect his guests (22:2; 19:8).

Genesis 2 tells of God creating Eve to be Adam's wife and of the first wedding. As God presents Eve to Adam, he cries out, "This at last is bone of my bones and flesh of my flesh; she shall be called Woman, because she was taken out of Man" (2:23). Every detail of this story is significant. It shows that marriage is more than a device for procreation, which we might have

9. S. Rimmon-Kenan, *Narrative Fiction: Contemporary Poetics* (London: Routledge, 1983), 120.

concluded had chapter 1 stood alone. Marriage is for companionship and mutual support. The animals were first created to
be man's companion, yet none of them matched him. Eve, created out of his rib, did match; she was a helper fit for him. That
is, they supported each other by complementing each other.

Commentators often have speculated as to why God chose to
make Eve out of Adam's rib rather than some other part of his
body. Matthew Henry evokes the spirit of the narrative when he
writes, "Not made out of his head to top him, not out of his feet
to be trampled upon by him, but out of his side to be equal with
him, under his arm to be protected, and near his heart to be beloved." Later, Adam himself refers back to Eve's origin, saying
that she is "bone of my bones and flesh of my flesh," a formula
used elsewhere of blood relatives (29:14). Applied to other marriages, this expresses the biblical conviction that marriage
makes spouses as close in relationship to each other as brother
and sister or parent and child. This has the consequence that
the relationship should be lifelong: "A man shall . . . hold fast to
his wife."

In Gen. 2, the Lord is portrayed as doing everything possible
for Adam's well-being, providing a well-watered garden full of
beautiful fruit trees. Noticing his loneliness, God creates all the
animals as Adam's companions, but they did not meet his need.
So eventually Eve is created. But is this not a bit mean? God
could have provided Adam with other men friends or several
Eves. That only one woman is provided by the all-powerful, all-
generous God surely is significant: it indicates the divine approval of heterosexual monogamy. One man with one woman
is God's model for relations between the sexes. Much of Genesis
shows the unhappiness caused by other arrangements. The first
bigamist is Lamech, the most vicious man in Genesis. Jacob's
involuntary bigamy and the tensions it aroused dominate the
second half of the book as Joseph, son of Rachel, antagonizes
his brothers, the sons of Leah and the slave girls. Similarly,
Hagar disrupted the harmony between Sarah and Abraham,
and Esau's wives made his parents' lives miserable. But the most
poignant comments are to be found in the naming of Leah's and
Rachel's children in Gen. 29–30. The names that Leah gave expressed the hope that her success in childbearing would make
her husband love her (29:32, 33, 34; 30:18, 20), whereas Rachel,

in naming Joseph, hoped that she would have another son
(30:24). It therefore seems highly likely that in relating the stories of the patriarchs' unhappy bigamous marriages, Genesis is
implicitly criticizing the arrangement. If, like Adam, they had
been content with just one wife, they might have enjoyed the relationship more.

But it was not merely that polygamy replaced monogamy
that caused these family problems. Genesis 3 onward shows
that the originally happy and innocent monogamous marriage
of Adam and Eve started to have its problems after they ate of
the forbidden fruit. Instead of being naked and unashamed,
they attempted to cover themselves with fig leaves and hide
among the trees of the garden (2:25; 3:7–8). The joy of their
original companionship was replaced by bickering as they tried
to blame someone else for their disobedience. Eve was designed to be a helper fit for Adam, but her actions in encouraging him to eat the fruit were hardly helpful. Later, Sarah per-
suaded Abraham to take Hagar as a surrogate mother, an
action that was perfectly respectable in the ancient Near East,
to ensure that he would have descendants and that the promise
would be fulfilled. However, Genesis criticizes this move by
using phraseology reminiscent of the account of the fall in Gen.
3, by showing the dissension it caused in the family, and finally
by describing the way it delayed the birth of a child to Sarah
herself.[10] Rebekah is also shown to be an unsuitable helpmeet
to Isaac when she instigated Jacob to deceive his father and her
husband in order to acquire the coveted firstborn's blessing.
Once again the consequences of her action are disastrous in
both the short term and the long: it provoked Esau to plan the
murder of his brother, and it forced Jacob to flee and, consequently, even if involuntarily, to marry both Leah and Rachel,
an act whose unhappy repercussions overshadow the rest of
Genesis.

However, it is not just wives who fail to live up to the ideals
set out in Gen. 2. As we saw, 2:24 sets out the paradigm for the
husband's behavior: "Therefore a man shall leave his father and
his mother and hold fast to his wife." This implies that a hus-

10. See Gordon J. Wenham, *Genesis 16–50*, WBC 2 (Dallas: Word, 1994), 6–
13.

band's first responsibility is to care for his wife, yet there are various situations in which the patriarchs fail in this duty. Twice Abraham failed to disclose that Sarah is his wife, so she was taken into the harem of a foreign king (12:10–20; 20:1–18). Isaac told the same story about Rebekah, but happily, she was not abducted (26:6–11). The Lord saw that Leah was hated (29:31), while Judah observed that Jacob never regarded her as his wife or his children as his own (44:27). So in this respect, the patriarchs fall short of the ideal set out in chapter 2.

And it is not just spouses who fail to live up to the divine ideals. Brothers kill each other (Cain and Abel) or plot to kill each other (Esau and Jacob, Joseph and his brothers). Children dishonor their parents: Ham and Noah, the daughters of Lot, and Reuben and Jacob, to give some of the clearest examples (9:22; 19:30–38; 35:22; 49:4). The Lord registers his bitter regret that "the intention of man's heart is evil from his youth" (6:5; 8:21), and in various ways the families of Genesis illustrate this truth.

The Message of the Pentateuch to Families

But this is not to say that the message of Genesis is essentially negative about families. Rather, it is a story of grace triumphing despite human sin, of grace triumphing even in families broken by sin. The book starts on a high note with the creation of the world climaxing with the creation of humankind in God's image and God declaring all that he had made was very good. The same optimistic outlook pervades chapter 2, and it is only in chapter 3 that things start to go wrong, with disobedience, dissension, and death replacing obedience, harmony, and life. Things get worse in chapter 4, with the emergence of fratricide and bigamy, and reach their nadir in chapter 6, where the earth is said to be full of violence (6:11, 13).

The flood destroyed the old creation, and the world was recreated and repopulated by the one perfect survivor of the old creation, Noah. But he too went astray, drinking too much wine; his son Ham sinned even worse, and eventually the building of the tower of Babel prompted another universal judgment.

But this is soon followed by the call of Abraham. He was summoned to leave home in Ur and promised four things: descendants, land, divine protection, and blessing on all the nations. As Clines has observed, these promises are "a reaffirmation of the primal divine intentions for man."[11] In other words, these promises assure Abraham that he and his descendants will begin to experience what Gen. 1–2 describes. Humankind was told to be fruitful and multiply; Abraham will have descendants as numerous as the stars of heaven. Adam was given the garden of Eden to till; Abraham is promised the land of Canaan flowing with milk and honey. In Eden, Adam and Eve enjoyed the continual presence and protection of God; Abraham and his descendants will enjoy similar blessing and protection. And ultimately, through Abraham and his offspring all the families of the world will find blessing.

The rest of Genesis elaborates these promises, making them richer and more comprehensive. It also shows their gradual but progressive fulfillment. The family of Abraham slowly and with great difficulty increased in number, so that there were seventy who actually went down to Egypt. In the course of their travels in Canaan, Abraham, Isaac, and Jacob acquired small portions of the land, such as wells, burial sites, and even a hilltop near Shechem. Throughout the sojourn they experienced God's protection and blessing, when they deserved it and when they did not. For although Genesis shows God's promises being enhanced after acts of faith and obedience (e.g., 13:14–17; 22:16–18), these promises are not nullified by disobedience; instead, their fulfillment is delayed (e.g., ch. 16). Ultimately, the promises rest on God's grace, not human obedience. Human obedience, the text implies, hastens the fulfillment of these promises and increases human happiness, but God never deserts those to whom he has made the promises.

These stories are not just the history of the giving of the promises and the origin of Israel and its claim to the land. They are that, of course, but they also are making an ethical appeal to their readers. The two longest stories in Genesis concern Jacob (chs. 25–35) and Joseph (chs. 37–50). Both tell of families rent apart by fratricidal hatred. Both tell of the cost to both sides in these disputes. Both climax with moving scenes of for-

11. D. J. A. Clines, *The Theme of the Pentateuch*, JSOTSup 10 (Sheffield: JSOT Press, 1978), 29.

giveness and reconciliation: "Esau ran to meet him, and embraced him, and fell on his neck and kissed him, and they wept" (Gen. 33:4 NRSV). Jacob responds by declaring, "I have seen your face, which is like seeing the face of God." Similarly, Joseph breaks down in tears as he declares, "I am Joseph! Is my father still alive?" (Gen. 45:3 NRSV).

This motif of reconciliation and forgiveness is evident elsewhere in Genesis. Abraham was anxious that his herdsmen and Lot's should not quarrel, and he put forward a generous proposal to solve the dispute (13:2–18). Later he and Isaac made treaties with Abimelech to stop the quarrel over wells (21:25–32; 26:26–33). Jacob expressed his anxiety that his sons' behavior would provoke the Canaanites to revenge (34:30). These examples of the patriarchs seeking peace and harmony within the Israelite family and with their neighbors in Canaan are enveloped by the opening and closing chapters of the book, which also picture the world at peace in Eden in chapter 2 and in Canaan in chapter 49. It therefore seems highly likely to me that Genesis is not merely recording the grace of God in calling Abraham and his descendants but also implicitly encouraging these descendants to follow their ancestors' examples by showing forgiveness and seeking reconciliation, however long and bitter former feuds have been. In this regard, the message of Genesis is relevant to all families in every time and space.

The Relevance of Pentateuchal Life Patterns Today

Can the actual pattern of family life described in Genesis be normative? Should we discourage mobility among our sons and encourage them to live near their parents? Should we arrange marriages for our daughters? Should adult males submit to their aged fathers? How should women relate to men today? These are some of the questions prompted by a study of families in the Pentateuch. And there are no easy answers, at least if we believe that "whatever was written in former days was written for our instruction" (Rom. 15:4 NRSV).

Nevertheless, I hope that my essay has pointed out some blind alleys. Genesis does suggest, on the one hand, that all human families, even the elect descendants of Abraham, are infected by sin and should not be imitated in every respect. On the other hand, Genesis implicitly puts forward a vision of a social order in which everyone cares for the other and lives in harmony with the other. The wife is a helper, matching her husband; the husband puts his wife's interest before anyone else's; children honor their parents; and so on. These principles may be applied, whatever the broader social pattern of family life may be.

It may be that we can go further. In discussing the social legislation of the Pentateuch (e.g., the Jubilee laws of Lev. 25), Christopher Wright has suggested that it may not be normative but paradigmatic.[12] That is, though these rules cannot be implemented in detail in modern society, we can, by examining their central objectives and ethos, discover values that we ought to emulate today. For example, we might not want to implement today the levirate law, which demanded that a widow marry her brother-in-law if she had no children. However, its concern to protect the fatherless family's capital and provide support for the widow should inform our legislation. Could the patterns of family life described in Genesis perhaps remind us of the value of family solidarity and the importance of putting the interests of the community before personal gain? Our children may not thank us if we offer to arrange marriages for them, but maybe we should pray harder that their choice will not be determined solely by chemistry or a soulless computer-dating agency! Of course, there are many more lessons we could learn from biblical society if we view it as paradigmatic, but these are just a few suggestions that have sprung to my mind.

12. Christopher J. H. Wright, *Living as the People of God* (Leicester, Eng.: Inter-Varsity, 1983); *God's People in God's Land: Family, Land, and Property in the Old Testament* (Grand Rapids: Eerdmans, 1990); *Walking in the Ways of the Lord: The Ethical Authority of the Old Testament* (Leicester, Eng.: Apollos; Downers Grove, Ill.: InterVarsity, 1995).

2

Family in the Non-narrative Sections of the Pentateuch

Edesio Sánchez

There is no question that family has been, still is, and will be an important topic in every field of human study, and religion is no exception. In today's society, and this is especially true in the United States, it is inconceivable to engage in the study of the current state of the family and ignore what the Christian and biblical traditions have to offer on this topic. With this purpose in mind, our theme for this book is "The Family in the Bible."

Even though I will try to cover most of the texts related to the family in the non-narrative sections of the Pentateuch (i.e., the Law), I will concentrate my presentation on Deuteronomy and the sections in that book that have to do with the home as the place for learning and living the biblical faith.

My travels throughout Latin American and my personal experience as part of a family, as a member of a congregation, and as a pastor lead me to affirm that the crisis many Christian denominations and churches are experiencing is due, in great measure, to the transference of teaching about faith and Christian life away from its rightful place, the home. My contention is that the home, not the church, is the center of vital teaching concerning our faith. The entire Bible is very clear about this.

The reasons why Christian parents have lost the opportunity to participate as key subjects in the training of their children are varied and complex. In the majority of cases, parents seem incapable of guiding their children through the labyrinths of life on the basis of biblical principles. Decisions concerning faith, morals, careers—to name only a few issues—have been left to schools, colleges, the mass media, schoolmates, or neighbors, and only in small measure to religious centers, much less to the home.

We must insist on a pastoral action that focuses all of its energies in such a way that the home becomes both the *subject* and the *object* of evangelization, humanization, and liberation. The role of religious centers is, above all, that of bringing families together for fellowship, sharing, and mutual ministry. Church membership must be understood, first of all, from the perspective of the component families and not as an aggregate of individuals. Before we speak of local churches or of parishes, we must speak of *the church in the home* (house churches or domestic churches). In his inaugural address at Puebla, the supreme head of the Roman Catholic Church said, "Make every effort so that there might be family pastoral action. Focus on this priority with the certainty that evangelization in the future will depend in large part on the church within the home."[1]

This essay is based on the assumption that the family, not simply the individual, is created in the image of God:

> Then God said, "Let us make humankind in our image, according to our likeness; and let them have dominion over the fish of the sea, and over the birds of the air, and over the cattle, and over all the wild animals of the earth, and over every creeping thing that creeps upon the earth." So God created humankind in his image, in the image of God he created them; male and female

1. Pope John Paul II, "Discurso inaugural," in *Puebla: III Conferencia General del Episcopado Latinoamericano, La Evangelización en el presente y el futuro de América Latina* (Bogotá, Colombia: Consejo Episcopal Latinoamericano, 1979), 31. See also Enrique Guang T., "La evangelización de la familia," in *CLADE II (Congreso Latinoamericano de Evangelización): América Latina y la Evangelización en los años 80* (n.p.: Fraternidad Teológica Latinoamericana, 1980), 67–73.

he created them. God blessed them, and God said to them, "Be
fruitful and multiply, and fill the earth and subdue it; and have
dominion over the fish of the sea and over the birds of the air
and over every living thing that moves upon the earth." (Gen.
1:26–28 NRSV)

This is the list of the descendants of Adam. When God created
humankind, he made them in the likeness of God. Male and female he created them, and he blessed them and named them
"Humankind" when they were created. When Adam had lived
one hundred thirty years, he became the father of a son in his
likeness, according to his image, and named him Seth. (Gen.
5:1–3 NRSV)

These two passages emphasize the creation of humanity as a
plurality—a community. From the beginning, that which is
created is not an individual but humankind, and this has its
basic nucleus in the family. These passages point out that the
divine image cannot be reduced to the individual as such but
applies to the created community (man-woman; man-woman-
child).

From the very opening of the great human drama, the Bible
clearly sets forth that every statement about humankind is a
statement concerning the family. When the Bible speaks about
humanity, it begins not with the individual but with the family,
with that essential community that is the raison d'être of the individual. From the outset of the human project, it is the family
that is foundational. The task of making human beings more
human and of turning the world into the "cosmos" of the Lord
has been committed to the family.

The Family in Ancient Israel and in the Pentateuch

Terminology for the Family in the Hebrew Bible

There are several important studies on the Hebrew terminology for the family. Norman Gottwald has provided one
such study from a sociological perspective. More recently, and
on the basis of advances in archaeological and ethnographic
research, Lawrence E. Stager, Carol Meyers, and others have

enriched and advanced studies by previous generations of scholars.

Joshua 7:14–18 (cf. Judg. 17–18) has become the *locus classicus* for understanding the use of the Hebrew words for family: *šēbet* ("tribe"), *mišpāḥâ* ("clan"), and *bayit* ("house"; or, better, *bêt-ʾāb*, "father's house"). With the help of ethnographic studies and archaeological research, these terms, especially the last two, can be understood as "kinship group" and "family household," respectively. In a more objective way, the "kinship group" can be understood as a small village, and the "family household" as the family compound or family unit, which lived in a "pillared house."[2]

Setting of the Family: The Village

The Israelite families that lived in the cities and villages of Iron Age I (beginning about 1200 B.C.E.) were located mostly in the hill country of Palestine (also known as Cisjordan). Archaeology has shown that the traditional idea that pastoral families (which tended flocks) lived in the highlands is wrong. Those who lived there were farmers, forming small unwalled settlements. As Carol Meyers writes,

> Just as an interplay of environmental influences and technological responses characterized Israel's pioneer period and helped shape social structures and values, so too did the hill country environment or ecosystem determine the nature of the agricultural system that the highland farmers established. The settlers chose crops suitable to the land and climate, and they developed technological strategies essential for making the land productive. The combination of environment and technology determined the needs and rhythms of agrarian life and thus the structure and size of the villages and their constituent families.[3]

2. Carol Meyers, "The Family in Early Israel," in *Families in Ancient Israel*, ed. L. G. Perdue et al., The Family, Religion, and Culture (Louisville: Westminster John Knox, 1997), 15–19; Lawrence E. Stager, "The Archaeology of the Family in Ancient Israel," *BASOR* 260 (1985): 18–23.

3. Carol Meyers, *Discovering Eve: Ancient Israelite Women in Context* (Oxford: Oxford University Press, 1988), 57.

Archaeological research has also shown that life in that place and time was harsh and difficult. The combination of a hard climate, disruption and social turmoil, and the constant threat of plagues and epidemic diseases made life exceedingly difficult. Consequently, it took the cooperation of all members of the household to survive and succeed. As the villages grew in number, and family and village life became more and more complex, laws and regulations needed to be developed for the well-being of the individual and the community.

Normally, a village was made up of extended families with a common ancestor. Therefore, villages had anywhere from around 50 to 150 people. The size of the villages ranged from half an acre to an acre.

The family household was formed by the senior couple, extended downward to include their children and grandchildren, and extended laterally to include other members of the family. The common family almost never exceeded fifteen. To these related members were added resident aliens, war captives, and servants. The average household also possessed tools, equipment, livestock, and orchards.

The Laws and Regulations for Family Living in the Pentateuch

One notices in the Old Testament, particularly in the Pentateuch, the care with which family life of Israel is regulated. All kinds of principles and laws needed to be formulated in order to regulate and maintain the family as the foundation of the people of God. The presence of the people of Israel among pagan cultures, as well as the way villages and family compounds were organized, required a genuine and well-thought-out family legislation. O. J. Babb observes, "The majority of the Biblical writers were vigorously opposed to forces that risked the integrity and security of the family, such as economic changes and the influence of foreign cultures and religions."[4] A long series of passages in the Pentateuch and the Wisdom liter-

4. O. J. Babb, "Family," *IDB* 2:238.

ature highlights the formulation of regulations for every level of family relations.[5]

Laws Related to Family Property

The survival of the family depended, in large measure, on the protection of the family property. If, as I noted, practically all villages were made up of related individuals, the alienation of property was a major threat to the well-being of the whole community; it meant, in fact, its destruction. Note the following texts:

> If anyone of your kin falls into difficulty and sells a piece of property, then the next of kin shall come and redeem what the relative has sold. If the person has no one to redeem it, but then prospers and finds sufficient means to do so, the years since its sale shall be computed and the difference shall be refunded to the person to whom it was sold, and the property shall be returned. But if there is not sufficient means to recover it, what was sold shall remain with the purchaser until the year of jubilee; in the jubilee it shall be released, and the property shall be returned. (Lev. 25:25–28 NRSV)

> No inheritance of the Israelites shall be transferred from one tribe to another; for all Israelites shall retain the inheritance of their ancestral tribes. Every daughter who possesses an inheritance in any tribe of the Israelites shall marry one from the clan of her father's tribe, so that all Israelites may continue to possess their ancestral inheritance. No inheritance shall be transferred from one tribe to another; for each of the tribes of the Israelites shall retain its own inheritance. (Num. 36:7–9 NRSV)

The property of the family could be passed only from parents to children, and in double proportion to the oldest son (Deut. 21:15–17). When there were no sons, the daughters inherited

5. Exod. 20:12 (cf. Deut. 5:16); 21:15, 17; Deut. 27:16; Lev. 20:9; Mal. 4:6; Ps. 44:1; 78:4–8; Prov. 1:8–9; 6:20–22; 10:1; 13:24; 15:5, 20, 32, 33; 30:17; 31:26; and many more). See H. W. Wolff, *Anthropology of the Old Testament*, trans. M. Kohl (London: SCM, 1974), 166–205; Roland de Vaux, *Ancient Israel*, vol. 1, *Social Institutions* (New York: McGraw-Hill, 1965); William Barclay, *Train Up a Child: Educational Ideals in the Ancient World* (Philadelphia: Westminster, 1959).

the paternal property (Num. 27:8–9), but they were not allowed to marry men from other tribes. And when there were no children at all, the closest relative inherited the property (Num. 27:9–11). The law of levirate marriage (Deut. 25:5–10) works in the same way: it protects family property.

Laws and Regulations Related to the Well-Being of the Household

If we keep in mind the picture of household compounds and the structure of the villages, it is easy to understand the value of the laws regarding the unity, health, and purity of the extended family. As Meyers notes, "The relatively large number of prohibited liaisons among consanguineal and affinal kin arises from the necessity to create taboos among the residents of an extended family household"[6] (see, e.g., the laws in Lev. 18 and 20).

The regulations on divorce (as androcentric as they might appear) also served to protect the integrity of the family. Some texts found in the Pentateuch indicate that "divorce was an arbitrary, unilateral, private act on the part of the husband and consisted of the wife's expulsion from the husband's house."[7] But in later times, as shown in Deut. 24:1–4, the husband was required to extend a bill of divorce to the wife at the time of the expulsion. This and other Deuteronomic laws (e.g., 22:13–24) show how a more humane and just attitude was taken on behalf of the most vulnerable of the society.

Regulations regarding slavery and the return of property given as a pledge until the return of the debt (Deut. 24:6, 10–15, 17–22) also reflect humane treatment. The regulations for the Sabbatical year and the Jubilee (Exod. 21:2–6; 23:6–11; Lev. 25; Deut. 15:1–18) are the greatest manifestation of justice and peace in a society governed by the word of God.

Roles and Functions within the Family

The need for survival in a harsh environment demanded that all members of the household compound participate in the

6. Meyers, "Family in Early Israel," 18.
7. Ze'ev W. Falk, *Hebrew Law in Biblical Times* (Winona Lake, Ind.: Eisenbrauns, 2001), 150.

tasks of daily life. As would be expected, adult members of the family undertook most of the important and difficult jobs. Children and the elderly also helped, but in lesser degree.

Some feminist scholars have shown that a patriarchal or androcentric society did not liberate women from numerous and difficult responsibilities at home and in the village. Besides the expected responsibilities of bearing and raising children, women engaged in tasks such as cleaning, grinding grain, food preparation and preservation, agricultural work, shepherding, producing textiles, basketry, ceramic production, and (on rare occasions) fighting in war and building. As Carol Meyers observes, "The boundaries of a woman's world were virtually the same as those of a man's in the highland hamlets of early Israel."[8] By comparing a woman's tasks with those of a man, we can conclude that women's work required greater technological expertise. So, it is with good reason that the Deuteronomist and the Wisdom writers exalted the key role women played in society (e.g., Prov. 31:11–31; several laws in Deuteronomy and stories in the Deuteronomistic literature give examples of this).

When looking at the relationship between parents and their children, one notices how the laws and regulations considered both parents equal. The same should be said of the Wisdom literature. The fifth commandment of the Decalogue gives guidelines for both children's and parental behavior. In order to better understand the message of such a commandment, we need to understand how the core cultural values of honor and shame worked in the ancient Mediterranean world.

From early childhood, children learned that respect and obedience were the best ways to honor their parents. And when they became adults and their parents were old, the commandment required them to take care of their parents in their elderly years. Sirach 3:1–16 conveys the spirit of the commandment:

> Listen to me your father, O children;
> act accordingly, that you may be kept in safety.
> For the Lord honors a father above his children,
> and he confirms a mother's right over her children.
> Those who honor their father atone for sins,

8. Meyers, "Family in Early Israel," 25.

and those who respect their mother are like those who lay up
treasure.
Those who honor their father will have joy in their own children,
and when they pray they will be heard.
Those who respect their father will have long life,
and those who honor their mother obey the Lord;
they will serve their parents as their masters.
Honor your father by word and deed,
that his blessing may come upon you.
For a father's blessing strengthens the houses of the children,
but a mother's curse uproots their foundations.
Do not glorify yourself by dishonoring your father,
for your father's dishonor is no glory to you.
The glory of one's father is one's own glory,
and it is a disgrace for children not to respect their mother.
My child, help your father in his old age,
and do not grieve him as long as he lives;
even if his mind fails, be patient with him;
because you have all your faculties do not despise him.
For kindness to a father will not be forgotten,
and will be credited to you against your sins;
in the day of your distress it will be remembered in your favor;
like frost in fair weather, your sins will melt away.
Whoever forsakes a father is like a blasphemer,
and whoever angers a mother is cursed by the Lord. (NRSV)

As a matter of fact, the fifth commandment seems to have been
written with a view to the grown children, who were required to
take care of elderly parents. Indeed, when one reads the commandment's promise with this idea in context, it is easier to
grasp its message: the integrity and well-being of the household
and villages would be kept for generations and generations.

The laws regarding the rebellious son (Deut. 21:18–21; cf.
Exod. 21:15, 17; Deut. 27:16) are set to give greater weight to
the commandment to honor parents. The Hebrew Bible and
rabbinic literature never mention the actual practice of such a
law. The main purpose of the law should be understood in this
way:

The punishment is not so much directed toward the son as towards the family. . . . The law has been constructed to prevent
parents abstaining from the duties of raising children and to
show them what is at loss here, namely the scarce commodity of

family honour, a status that can be displayed by having a wise son that listens to his father's discipline.[9]

Consequently, the fifth commandment also puts a burden on the parents: to gain the right to be honored by their children. When the father or the mother is placed on the "scale" of such a challenge, how much does each "weigh"?

In the second part of this essay, I concentrate on what Deuteronomy as a whole and 6:4–9 as a unit teach us about building a family according to God's word. The texts that affirm the family as the center for religious instruction stand out among the laws and regulations in Deuteronomy. As a religious community, the family preserved the traditions of the past and transmitted them by means of instruction and worship.[10] The central feast in the Old Testament, the Passover, was a family festival, which took place in the home. The entire context of the ritual was the home, and it was the father who presided. In the midst of the celebration, at the moment of the "second cup," one of the sons would ask, "Why is this night different from others?" The question opened up the opportunity for the father to narrate the historical redemption of the people from the hand of the Egyptians. This practice was cultivated and transmitted from generation to generation. Jesus and his contemporaries followed the same practice.[11]

The Family in Deuteronomy

The Context of the Book

Before taking a closer look at Deuteronomy, we should consider its literary and historical context. It is worthwhile to note that Deuteronomy has played a vital role in the development of biblical faith. It makes its appearance as the textbook and basis for theological reflection during the great moments of the history of Israel (Josiah's reformation; the exile). In fact, this book

9. Anselm C. Hagedorn, "Guarding the Parents' Honour—Deuteronomy 21:18–21," *JSOT* 88 (2000): 115.

10. Babb, "Family," 238.

11. J. C. Rylaarsdam, "Passover and Feast of Unleavened Bread," *IDB* 3:665.

provided the theological foundations for the creation of the monumental historical work of the Deuteronomist (from Joshua to 2 Kings).[12] This book is the standard for evaluating the history of the people, the priests, and the kings of Israel. It is one of the most popular books in the extensive Qumran literature and one of the most heavily quoted books in the New Testament (eighty-three times). Several contemporary Bible scholars would agree that "the book of Deuteronomy stands at the heart of Biblical theology. . . . A theology of the Old Testament must take Deuteronomy as its center because it is there where the basic elements of an Old Testament theology are concentrated."[13]

Herein lies the great value of Deuteronomy. It evidences itself as a book that, having gathered the word of God, makes that word come alive for the benefit of a new people, a new generation. Deuteronomy is a clear indication of an indisputable fact in the biblical message: whatever changes there might be as to moment, history, and audience, the word of God is the same. Deuteronomy is an example of a correct hermeneutic, in which the word and the historical context meet each other in a responsible dialogue—a dialogue in which due recognition is given to the fact that the word speaks its message only when it injects itself into the context of the hearer and speaks to him or her from there. The purpose of the book is to draw near to a new generation, in a specific historical situation, in order to explain the law. For this reason it was necessary to recapitulate, retell, and explain what had gone before as well as what was taking place "here and now."[14]

The book speaks about the law, but not from a juridical point of view. It is not a book written for judges and priests. It was written with all of the people of Israel in mind—not for usage in a court of law, but in the home.[15] That is why we find, alongside the commands to obey the law, the insistence upon its

12. See Martin Noth, *The Deuteronomistic History*, JSOTSup 15 (Sheffield: JSOT Press, 1981).

13. Gerhard Hasel, *Old Testament Theology: Basic Issues in the Current Debate*, rev. ed. (Grand Rapids: Eerdmans, 1975), 95–96.

14. Brevard S. Childs, *Introduction to the Old Testament as Scripture* (Philadelphia: Fortress, 1979), 212.

15. G. Ernest Wright, "The Book of Deuteronomy," *IDB* 2:312.

teaching and instruction (4:1, 5, 9, 10, 14, 39; 5:1, 31; 6:1, 7–10; 11:18–20). In fact, this didactic use of the book does justice to the basic meaning of the term *torah:* the law is not simply a corpus of regulations; it is, in a special way, faith being taught; it is instruction.[16] The subjects of this teaching are the parents. They must teach their children in the ways and word of the Lord. There is no other book in the Bible that makes instruction to children and youth so central to the message as does Deuteronomy (4:9; 6:7, 20–25; 11:19; 31:13; etc.).[17]

Several important elements relate to the purpose of this book. First, let us look at the "generational" factor. It is noteworthy how Deuteronomy weaves into its narration constant references to the people of "yesterday," "today," and "tomorrow," and "your ancestors," "you," and "your children" (1:35, 38–39; 4:9, 25; 5:2–3, 29; 6:2–3; 7:9; 8:1, 16; 9:5; 10:11, 15; 11:2, 7, 19, 21; 29:10, 14–15, 22, 29). Deuteronomy has a different attitude toward each generation. "Yesterday's" generation is on trial (1:39; 4:1–9, 15–20). The people of "tomorrow," depending on the teaching they receive "today," could either be unfaithful (4:25–28) or faithful and obedient (4:29–31, 39–40; 5:32–33). The relationship of the people with God will depend on the people's quality of life. The Lord expects obedience and faithfulness. According to Deuteronomy, the quality of life for future generations will depend to a great degree on the lifestyle of the present generation (6:1–3).

Second, along with the generational theme, there also appears the temporal concept "today."[18] Jacques Briend describes it this way:

The term expresses with unequaled force the profound perception that the action of God places itself within the concrete ex-

16. William L. Holladay, *A Concise Hebrew and Aramaic Lexicon of the Old Testament* (Grand Rapids: Eerdmans, 1971), 388.

17. Elizabeth Achtemeier, *Deuteronomy, Jeremiah,* Proclamation Commentaries (Philadelphia: Fortress, 1978), 13.

18. "In the sections framing the Deuteronomic Code (4:44–30:20) *hayyôm* (today) is to be found 35 times and *hayyôm hazzeh* (this day) 6 times; in addition, in the body of the Code itself (chs. 12–26) *hayyôm* occurs 9 times and *hayyôm hazzeh* once. All in all *hayyôm* is found 58 times in the book of Deuteronomy and *hayyôm hazzeh* 12 times; that is to say, 'today' is found 70 times in all" (Wolff, *Anthropology of the Old Testament,* 86–87).

istence of the people. The place that this term occupies in Deuteronomy is evidence that the concept of temporality that appears in the document is the same from beginning to end. Every generation of Israel must witness God's actions and Word: "Hear, O Israel, the statutes and judgments which I speak in your ears this day" (5:1; cf. 5:3, 24). In this way, every generation is made to share in the work of God, which is established in a today that depends totally upon him. Before the Word of God, all are called to obey, to put into practice and to keep his word in their hearts (6:6) so that it might serve as a guide in the path to happiness.[19]

The word of God, given to God's people through a covenant, always speaks to humankind today. It invites those who are in the "now" to look at "yesterday" (which, according to Deuteronomy, is the history of a rebellious people, of Moses' intercession, and of new divine reconciliation). "Yesterday" can be forgotten only at the risk of suffering "tomorrow's" consequences even "today" (8:19).[20] Though it draws attention to the times of their ancestors for those of today's generation, who are the heirs of a historical tradition, Deuteronomy insists that the generation of today is largely responsible for the future. Therefore, constant appeals are made to those who are listening today: "remember," "see that you do not forget" (6:12; 8:19). To forget is to sin against faith and hope. Consequently, it is necessary to attend to the word that is spoken today, to reflect upon how their ancestors put it into practice, to be vigilant, and to decide for the future (29:29).[21] "Today" is not only now; it is also "tomorrow" (29:14–15). The covenant confirms this. The renewed covenant at Moab, Shechem, and Jerusalem is an invitation to mold the future out of today's dialogue. We take hold of the covenant and of its Lord in order to be assured of the future.

Third, if our purpose is to explain the law to a new generation in a new situation, there is no better literary form than the homiletical approach.[22] The contents of the book are couched

---

19. Jacques Briend, *El Pentateuco*, Cuadernos Bíblicos 13 (Estella, Spain: Editorial Verbo Divino, 1978), 45 (my translation).

20. Wolff, *Anthropology of the Old Testament*, 87.

21. Ibid., 88.

22. See the use of *bʾr* ("explain") in Deut. 1:5; 27:8. See Childs, *Old Testament as Scripture*, 212.

in terms of an urgent appeal, which is why the style is homiletical. All of the attempts to structure Deuteronomy as a suzerainty treaty end up doing acrobatics that artificially separate the book from its essential purpose. It is true that these treaties exerted some influence, in form as well as in vocabulary, but Deuteronomy is not, as such, a treaty document. The book is set forth as a series of discourses or sermons to a people who were standing before their leader as he bid them farewell.[23] Any reference to the suzerainty treaties is intended to highlight the fact that today's generation, the same as yesterday's, is tied to the covenant. Thus, the homiletical style and the suzerainty treaty structure are interwoven with other elements to point out that Deuteronomy is so ordered that it might always remain relevant for each new generation of Israel.

Deuteronomy is a book for a people in transition (a nation threatened by temptations and disasters), for a generation whose task is to conquer and build a new land, a new society. It is a book that, like Matthew in the New Testament, is intended as a manual for members of the kingdom of God. (How pertinent it is for this big country today!)

The book is made up of five sections, which can be better understood if they are placed in concentric circles. In the innermost circle stand chapters 12–26, which contain the covenant laws.[24] In the next circle are chapters 5–11 and 27–30, which locate the legal code in the context of the new situation that is now being experienced. The section made up of chapters 5–11 begins with the Sinai theophany, followed by the Decalogue, both of which are decisive elements in God's covenant with Israel. Thus, before the legal code (chs. 12–26) is presented to those of this new generation, they are made to participate in the covenant. This event from the past is now placed in an introductory section, which is bracketed by the term "today." Like-

23. See A. D. H. Mayes, *Deuteronomy*, NCB (London: Oliphants, 1979), 33–34; E. W. Nicholson, *Deuteronomy and Tradition* (Philadelphia: Fortress, 1967), 46; Dean McBride, "The Yoke of the Kingdom: An Exposition of Deuteronomy 6:4–5," *Int* 27, no. 3 (1973): 273–306, esp. 288. Cf. J. G. McConville, *Deuteronomy*, Apollos Old Testament Commentary (Leicester, Eng.: Apollos; Downers Grove, Ill.: InterVarsity, 2002), 42–43.

24. According to most biblical scholars, this is the oldest section of the book.

The Five Sections of Deuteronomy

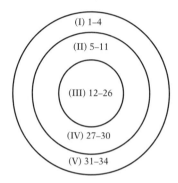

wise, at the end of the chapters 5–11 section are two almost parallel passages that insist that the responsibility for teaching the precepts of faith belongs to the home and particularly to parents (6:4–9—a text that is in the same section as the story of the Sinaitic covenant, 11:18–20). Chapters 27–30 are set forth as the conclusion of the Deuteronomic code.[25]

The outermost circle contains sections I (chs. 1–4) and V (chs. 31–34).[26] The role of chapters 1–4 is to recapitulate the history of the past generation and to confront the present generation with a new beginning. They make up the prologue of the book, and together with section II (chs. 5–11), they answer the question "How does the old relate to the new?"[27] The first section reminds us of the judgment of the past generation; the second offers a challenge to the new generation.

The fifth section is placed at the conclusion of the entire book. Chapter 31 describes Moses' final actions: he finishes his sermon and sets it down in writing, commissions Joshua, deposits the law next to the ark, and establishes the practices of the reading of the law. Chapter 32 (a poem) is a prophetic presentation in which Moses speaks about God's faithfulness in contrast to the rebellion of the people. In this poem Moses brings together the three generations. Chapter 33 (also a

25. Childs, *Old Testament as Scripture*, 219.

26. According to Noth (*Deuteronomistic History*, 31, 35), both appear largely during the exile; cf. Achtemeier, *Deuteronomy, Jeremiah*, 19.

27. Childs, *Old Testament as Scripture*, 214–15.

poem) outlines, in prophetic terms, a future ideal situation: the kingdom of God. Chapter 34 strikes the final note: a leader passes away (past generation), and a new leader appears (new generation).[28]

Deuteronomy 6:4–9

The suggestions and general observations made concerning our main topic point to, and radiate from, Deut. 6:4–9. Here we find this theme explicitly dealt with within the context of the most categorical of all statements about Yahweh, the Lord: the Shema. Deuteronomy cannot find a more important place to deposit the core of biblical faith than in the home.

These verses belong to a more extensive unit (6:4–25) at the end of which we find a clearly pedagogical family dialogue: the parent is responding to a question that has been posed by a child. Verses 4–9 constitute the more ancient portion.[29] Of these verses, the first two (4–5) are the axis upon which the entire unit hinges. In fact, and without exaggeration, the whole book is a commentary on these two verses.[30] McBride says of Deuteronomy 6:4–5, "There is no other passage that captures with greater eloquence the spirit that suffuses the book of Deuteronomy."[31]

Deuteronomy 6:4–9 is structured in such a way that all that is declared and commanded is built upon the unit principle. In v. 6, the phrase "these words" (or commandments) serves as a link, as well as an emphatic statement.[32] With this phrase the author ties in each element in the unit. Verbs, pronouns, and

28. Ibid., 219.

29. Gerhard von Rad, along with others, points out that the exhortations found here, especially the parts written in the second person singular, belong to the original strata of Deuteronomy.

30. Gerhard von Rad, *Studies in Deuteronomy*, trans. D. Stalker, Studies in Biblical Theology 9 (London: SCM Press, 1953), 71; Nicholson, *Deuteronomy and Tradition*, 46.

31. McBride, "Yoke of the Kingdom," 288.

32. Félix García López points out that when, in Hebrew, the term "words" (commands) is preceded by the demonstrative "these," it always refers to any concrete object that has been presented in the preceding immediate context ("Deut VI et la Tradition-Rédaction du Deutéronome," *RB* 86, no. 2 [1979]: 59–91, esp. 72–76).

articles are virtually swept along toward the unifying principle: "Hear, O Israel: The LORD is our God, the LORD alone. You shall love the LORD your God with all your heart, and with all your soul, and with all your might" (NRSV).[33] Everything that is said in Deut. 6:6–9 has value only in relation to this nucleus (6:4–5) that intimately links a "dogmatic" affirmation (v. 4b) and an "ethical-religious" demand (v. 5a).

With the words "The LORD is our God, the LORD alone," the author expresses positively the first commandment of the Decalogue. Israel is confronted once more with the singularity of the Lord.[34] This declaration can be understood only when we locate it in the historical, political, and religious context of the Deuteronomic tradition. Every time that past history is related, the point is made that Israel lives solely because Yahweh directs its life. The Lord governs Israel. The life of Israel depends on its recognition of Yahweh as its sovereign. This is why the author is deeply concerned about the temptations that the people will face in Canaan—so many gods to worship, so many high places in which to gather, so many different practices in which to become involved!

A logical consequence of our recognition of the Lord's oneness is our complete love for God. If we recognize only one God, then our love will be only for Yahweh. Love of God in the Old Testament is part of the context of the covenant. The love that is required of Israel is "payment in the same coin," because it is a response that is commensurate with the faithfulness of God, who always holds to and fulfills his promises (Deut. 4:37; 10:15; 7:7–8). Israel is invited to love because God loved Israel first (cf. 1 John 4:19). The first fruit of divine love in Deuteronomy is obedience.[35] Deuteronomy is the first book to utilize extensively the

33. The principal verbs, all of them in the future indicative, are syntactically united to the first verb (in the imperative) by means of the conjunction "and" (*waw*). This sequence, in accordance with Hebrew grammar, causes all of the indicative verbs to be understood as imperatives. See Thomas O. Lambdin, *Introduction to Biblical Hebrew* (New York: Charles Scribner's Sons, 1971), 119. Accordingly, the Good News Bible (TEV) translates all of these verbs as imperatives.

34. In fact, all of Deuteronomy and the work of the Deuteronomist rest upon the belief in the total uniqueness of the relationship between Yahweh and his people: one God, one sanctuary, one law, one land, one people.

35. Wright, "Book of Deuteronomy," 373.

theme of human love for God,[36] and it develops this concept in the context of the family. Yet we are not speaking here of mere feelings. We are referring to a love that reasons, which is why it can be presented in the form of a command. This is the love that children owe their parents, the synonym of which is obedience.

Verses 5b–7 follow the requirement in v. 5a and emphasize the idea of totality and perfection. The nouns "heart," "soul," and "might" make up the totality of a human being: mind, personality, and worth. The word "all," thrice repeated, insists upon the perfection and intensity of the love commitment. Everything that makes up the human person is presented here as the seat of divine love. In v. 7, the idea of totality is shown through the use of two polar contrasts: "sit/walk" and "lie down/ rise up." These four verbs cover every daily human activity.[37] The human person, in the totality of his or her existence, lives to love only one God, Yahweh.

The themes of the singularity of Yahweh, our undivided love for this God, and the fight against other gods and idols appear at each step of the Deuteronomic literature (Deuteronomy, Joshua, Judges, 1–2 Samuel, 1–2 Kings). In fact, each time the Deuteronomist evaluates the different stages of the history of Israel, the approval or rejection of the people or of their leaders depends on their undivided loyalty, or lack of it, to the Lord. Deuteronomy 6:10–25 speaks categorically to this issue: "The LORD your God you shall fear; him you shall serve, and by his name alone you shall swear. Do not follow other gods, any of the gods of the peoples who are all around you" (vv. 13–14 NRSV).[38]

Beginning with the Decalogue, the commandment against idolatry is elaborated within a family context:

> You shall not make for yourself an idol, whether in the form of anything that is in heaven above, or that is on the earth beneath, or that is in the water under the earth. You shall not bow down

36. It has been called the biblical document of love par excellence. See W. L. Moran, "The Ancient Near Eastern Background of the Love of God in Deuteronomy," *CBQ* 25, no. 1 (1963): 77–87.

37. García López, "Deut VI et la Tradition-Rédaction de Deutéronomie," 77–78.

38. Cf. Deut. 4:3, 15–40; 5:7–10; 7:4–5, 16, 25; 8:19; 9:12, 16; 10:20–21; 11:16, 28; 27:15; 28:14; 29:17–18, 26.

to them or worship them; for I the LORD your God am a jealous
God, punishing children for the iniquity of parents, to the third
and fourth generation of those who reject me, but showing
steadfast love to the thousandth generation of those who love
me and keep my commandments. (Deut. 5:8–10 NRSV; cf. Exod.
20:4–6)

Deuteronomy 6:4–9 makes this theme even more explicit. Time
and again, in the context of the teaching dialogue at home
(Deut. 6:20–25; 11:18–32; 29:29–30:10; cf. 4:9–10; 6:1–3), Israel
is reminded to be faithful to Yahweh alone.

Although it is true that this law is given in the context of worship before the entire assembly of Israel (Exod. 19–24; Josh. 24;
2 Kings 22–23), Deuteronomy time and again makes it clear
that the primary relationship of this commandment is within
the boundaries of the family, the home. Even in the context of
the assembly of the people, there is always a reference to parents and children (Exod. 20; Deut. 5; 6:4–7; 30) or to the family
(Josh. 24:15). Faithfulness to the Lord and teaching in the family go hand in hand. It is no accident that in those periods of unfaithfulness and apostasy, the homes of the protagonists were
deemed bankrupt (Judg. 14–16; 1 Sam. 2:12, 17, 22–25, 29–36;
3:13–14; 4:17–22; 1 Kings 11; 2 Kings 21:6). Furthermore, the
Deuteronomist does not hold back from stamping his bitter critique upon family life, even of those whom he calls faithful servants of the Lord (1 Sam. 8:1–5; 2 Sam. 12–1 Kings 1).

There can be no doubt that the Deuteronomist always kept
in mind Deut. 6:4–9 when he wrote the history of Israel from exodus to exile. Throughout the whole of the Deuteronomic literature, it has been made clear that the disasters of the "present"
were due to Israel's not having been able to obey the central
teachings of the covenant at home: undivided loyalty and total
love to Yahweh.

We must not, therefore, lose sight of the starting point of any
study concerning the family. Every study on family in the Bible
must begin from this central principle: the Lord is our God alone.
According to our passage, immediately after the presentation of
that basic element (that in itself is the content of faith and teaching) comes the presentation of the pedagogical steps—what do we
expect to happen in the community of the people of God? It is in-

teresting to note the transition from the collective and general ("Israel") to the individual and concrete ("your heart," "your house," "your sons"), and once more to the general ("your gates"—meaning the whole town or city). What is presented here is a life program that maintains a good balance between the community and the individual, with the home as the fulcrum.

We find in our passage a triple pedagogical commitment: (1) to oneself ("Keep these words that I am commanding you today in your heart"), (2) toward children ("Recite them to your children"), and (3) toward the community ("Write them . . . on your gates"). It is obvious that the teaching commitment is concentrated primarily in the home. Verses 7 and 9 make the home the environment where "these commandments" will be the object of both teaching and practice. Verses 20–25 speak about this in terms of a pedagogical interaction: the child addresses a question to the parent, and the parent in turn responds by narrating the mighty acts of the Lord in the past and by stating God's demands for the future.

The following scheme highlights the pedagogical emphasis of the text:

The teaching received:	"Hear . . . these words" (vv. 4, 6).
The teaching practiced:	"Keep these words" (v. 6).
The teaching passed on:	"Repeat them to your children" (v. 7).
The teaching reviewed:	"Recite them . . . bind them . . . write them" (vv. 7–9).

Our passage masterfully weaves together the what and the how—the content and the process of teaching. In this passage we find both the subjects and the receptors of the teaching: parents and children; the content: "these commandments"; and the form: oral, written, and practical communication.

Lessons for Today

Two facts stand out in all this: the content and the place of teaching about our faith (life). Both elements are crucial for today. When we take them seriously within our contemporary practice, our pastoral perspectives and projects will take a 180-degree turn. The urgent need for change grows when we place, alongside these biblical demands, the condition of the so-called Christian family of our times. It is not possible in our day to draw a clear-cut distinction between lifestyle, training, practices, and priorities of Christian and non-Christian families. That romantic belief that we Christians live far above "worldly concerns" has been shattered. In fact, it has never been true!

Make a simple inventory of the formative experiences in the life of a family. You will find that the content of family training is, for the most part, beyond our control. The purposes and the goals are removed from—and, more often than not, set against—biblical faith. When we compare this with the quality and time dedicated to teaching on the Christian life, we cannot expect more than an exceedingly poor impact from the latter upon individuals and communities. The homogenizing culture of the communication media has broken down the limits set by social class, geographical distances, and levels of academic training. We are living in the midst of a system that has "omnipresent" power, whose philosophy of life virtually reaches all of us: materialism, consumerism, individualism, and hedonism.

We must develop a family pastoral action that maintains a balance between biblical teaching and the historical circumstances in which our families develop. What is taught and where it is taught are the central elements in this study, which can serve as guidelines for such a pastoral action because they offer us a "front line of attack" against the forces of the worldview of the system in which we live.

Theology: The Content of Teaching

The biblical affirmation "The LORD is our God, the LORD alone. You shall love the LORD your God with all your heart, and with all your soul, and with all your might" (Deut. 6:4–5) speaks to us today with the same ethical and dogmatic authority. It states a principle and a demand of perennial value. The variable is the historical-geographical elements within which it is applied in every age.

It is urgent that we develop the discourse concerning God in the context of the living experience of our own communities, be these in the United States or Latin America. We need to rediscover in Scripture what defines this God and Lord and the acts of grace and judgment of our Lord that are hostile to so many gods, idols, and fetishes. In this way we can have at our disposal guidelines for today to help us differentiate between God the Lord and the false gods. Concepts such as "knowledge of God" and "idolatry" need to be restudied, both from the Bible and in our contemporary society.[39]

False Scripture interpretations and theological tendencies populate the "faith system" of our people. What we need is to draw our people closer to that distant God (who is "way out there") so that God might free us from the "Christs" of our popular religiosities! What we most need is to "unmask" all of the impostor gods that are being offered under the "name" of God—those false lifestyles, as well as our muzzled religion, which have become the servant of a materialistic and dehumanizing economic system.[40]

It is impossible to develop in this essay the general ideas that I have expressed. I have referred to them only to underscore our need to maintain a good balance between the what and the where of our teaching concerning the Christian faith. Both dimensions are basic and indivisible. The development of a Christian education strategy within the home, without the input from a trustworthy theology, is unworkable. The same thing happens when we are concerned only with developing a sound

39. Several studies have already appeared concerning this subject. See José Porfirio Miranda, *Marx and the Bible: A Critique of the Philosophy of Oppression*, trans. J. Eagleson (Maryknoll: Orbis, 1974); José Luis Sicre, *Los dioses olvidados: Poder y riqueza en los profetas preexílicos* (Madrid: Cristiandad, 1979); Pablo Richard et al., *La lucha de los dioses: Los ídolos de la opresión y la búsqueda del Dios Liberador* (San José, Costa Rica: DEI, 1978). Nevertheless, the task is still in the discovery and development phase. We still need works that are written at a more popular level with our churches in mind.

40. Several monographs and studies have appeared in Latin America and the United States that refer to the false gods, idols, and fetishes of the system. See José Míguez Bonino, *Espacio para ser hombre* (Buenos Aires: Tierra Nueva, 1975); Rubén Alvez, *Tomorrow's Child* (New York: Harper & Row, 1972); W. Stringfellow, *An Ethic for Christians and Other Aliens in a Strange Land* (Waco, Tex.: Word, 1973).

and evangelical theology while we overlook the home, which should be its main locus. It is obvious that the best theological reflection is not reaching the members of the churches, much less the home. Meanwhile, our families are bombarded by the idolatrous systems of our contemporary world via the mass media, which convey the values and "theology" of films and soap operas, as well as the worldview and priorities set by commercials. A large number of churches and homes have built their faith upon the anti-theology of "fiction theology" (pop theology) and upon a "cheap" gospel, which is largely being offered in so-called Christian bookstores.

Just as it is necessary to develop a teaching strategy within the home, it is also urgent to develop a trustworthy biblical and theological content for Christian education.

The Home: The Place for Christian Teaching

Two apparently contradictory facts were presented in a joint study on *The Family as Educator:*[41]

1. "In our society we cannot look upon the family as a closed system. It must be seen as a system which is open to a multiplicity of external influences. . . . When we take into account the time that family members spend inside and outside the home, it immediately becomes clear that it is a fallacy to consider the family as the source of all the significant influences."[42]

2. "The home is an arena where virtually all of the range of human experiences can take place. . . . Parents would do well to look out for the training of their children because it is in the home where the first and most lasting influences are produced. . . . For better or for worse, we must all recognize that within the home a rich variety of training encounters take place: arguments, violence, love, tactfulness, honesty, deceit, a sense of private property, community participation, manipulation, group decision, 'power

41. Hope J. Leichter, ed., *The Family as Educator* (New York: Teachers College Press, 1974).
42. Ibid., 25–26.

centers,' equality, etc. All of this can happen within the home."[43]

Nevertheless, these realities are not exclusive. External influences are always filtered through family members and do not take place in a vacuum. The values and anti-values of life reach our children—and family members in general—through the parents, whether directly or indirectly. In fact, the most influential teachings are the attitudes and practices, and very little the "speeches" or "sermons," of parents. How often parents are upset about the low impact of their words! With sorrow they discover the reason: their words contradict their attitudes and practices. Children suffer from a contradictory parental pedagogy. On the one hand, they perceive our nonverbal communication, our attitudes and actions; on the other hand, they are aware of the countercommands, the verbal communication concerning what a child must or must not do.

A certain mother, who suffered from seeing the wayward lives of her two adolescent daughters, said to me, "Why have they done this to us? Haven't we been concerned about teaching them the ways of the Lord?" And it was true. This was one of those families whose "faithfulness" was evident even in the practice of family devotions. They were involved in most of their church's activities. Nonetheless, a conversation with the entire family revealed the other pole of the problem. There was a conscious communication: "Go to church, read the Bible"; but there was also the other communication: the relationship between the parents, their contact with their daughters, the values that were instilled by way of the "nonreligious" practices that took place outside of the "religious" activities, permissive discipline, television, and undiscriminating reading practices in the home.

It is here that Deut. 6:4–9 can lend us a hand in setting guidelines that help us in our search for a solution. As was the case in the particular historical moment of our Scripture passage, our present situation points to the home as being the most logical place for training in the Christian life. It is here that intergenerational relationships are more spontaneous and signifi-

43. Ibid., 1, 3, 9.

cant, and the teaching opportunities are the most varied and rich. The home provides us with the opportunity to be taught "academically," as well as by experience and example. Though it is true that parents are the principal training subjects, a wide gamut of similar opportunities opens up for the other family members. More time is spent at home than in the religious instruction centers. In the home, even the most academic and "abstract" doctrine has a chance of becoming a challenge and a lifestyle.

We need to recognize that every attempt to maintain the church building and Sunday as *the* place and *the* time of training for Christian living has failed and will continue to do so. Classic Christian education has shown itself incapable of being obedient to the biblical command and providing answers for existential needs. A line of communication has been stretched between theological centers and the home that passes through the church. This is an intellectual and theoretical Christian education. All that is needed is a glance at curricula of the majority of our seminaries in order to recognize this. Seminaries and churches, teachers and pastors, have become repositories of the educational system of the schools and universities of today's world. What is deemed important is information, not formation (training). Curricula and classes have been divided in the Sunday school according to age groups. Weekly activities generally are programmed with different age groups and sexes in mind: women's and men's groups, youth and preteen groups, and children's classes. In the majority of our churches the Sunday morning service is designed to exclude children. Is there any significant activity in our churches that involves the entire family? Generally speaking, the answer is no. In the face of such a structure it is not difficult to understand why parents find so many problems "transmitting" at home the beliefs that they learn in church. The biblical view has been lost. The church building ought not to be the seedbed of the Christian life. That role belongs to the home.

What, then, shall we do? Here are some principles to follow, which take into account the guidelines that were established in the passage in Deuteronomy:

1. The membership of any church is made up, primarily, of families, not of individuals. Therefore, the church should be structured with families in mind and not only individuals. Thus, the family unit should be seen as the fundamental focus of mission and diaconate— families serving other families, families evangelizing families.

2. This structure takes the centrality of the family seriously as both the pedagogical subject and object. This means that enough time should be allowed to teach and orient family cells. Likewise, the curriculum should be planned with these family cells in mind, providing materials that will help Christians to develop their faith first of all within the home.

3. When we understand Christian education in this way, the upbringing of children becomes primarily a parental responsibility. Parents are the most effective co-pastors. Thus, teaching is no longer simply an intellectual exercise; it becomes the developer of a responsible life, instilling biblical values, as well as a disciplinary instrument lovingly applied. Parents themselves are challenged to become mature Christians. This is training *in* life that prepares people *for* life.

4. This perspective helps us to understand and to experience more readily the pedagogical principle found in Deut. 6:4–9. "These commands" are the object of Christian teaching within the total environment of daily life. Thus, to be a Christian is no longer the result of an intellectual affirmation, of a creedal statement, or of a Sunday-only activity in a fixed locality. It becomes a lifestyle—a new life—that becomes all the more evident at the most secular and profane hours of daily life. To be Christian is to live in submission to the Lord, and only to him, twenty-four hours a day.

5. When we make the family the foundation of our ecclesiastical structure, our programming of activities and experiences by age, gender, and academic level will become more significant. The lines of our interpersonal relationships will be enriched when we permit a wide variety of experiences, both generational and intergenerational.

6. This kind of family-oriented ecclesial life will encourage us to look forward to the Sunday service as a family worship celebration in which no one should feel left out. The Lord's Supper will then recover its biblical basis and meaning.

3

Family in the Historical Books

DAVID T. TSUMURA

The Historical Books of the Old Testament are full of interesting stories of family affairs. Some are good and beautiful, as the stories of Naomi and Ruth,[1] and Elkanah and Hannah; others are unpleasant and painful, as those of Eli's sons, Samuel, David, and Josiah. It is noteworthy that these religious and political leaders in ancient Israel failed in the upbringing of their own sons. Even though they were great leaders in society, they were not good fathers.[2]

However, the Book of Joshua, the first of the Historical Books, begins and ends with characters who display positive concern toward their families—the former, an unexpected female leader of a family; the latter, the head of a normal family in ancient Israel. In Josh. 2:12, Rahab, though a prostitute, "a social outcast, who was generally forced into the profession by destitution or loss of

1. The Book of Ruth is treated here as a historical book, though the Hebrew Bible classifies it as belonging to the Writings.
2. For a good summary on the family in the Old Testament, see C. J. H. Wright, "Family," *ABD* 2:761–68.

parents or spouse,"[3] asks Israelite spies to show kindness to her
family when they attack Jericho. Then, in the final chapter of the
book, Joshua, the leader of the covenant people Israel, exhorts
them to "fear the Lord and serve him in sincerity and in truth"
(24:14). But even if they choose other gods, Joshua declares, "As
for me and my household [wĕʾānōkî ûbêtî], we will serve the
Lord" (24:15). Joshua managed well not only his people as their
leader but also his family as head of his household.

Kinship Structure in Ancient Israel

In these episodes we notice the use of different Hebrew ex-
pressions for the family. While Joshua uses the term "household" (bêt; lit., "house") to refer to his family, in 2:12 Rahab uses
the expression bêt ʾābî (lit., "the house of my father") for her
family. In the next verse, she paraphrases it as "my father and
mother, my brothers and sisters, and all who belong to them."
The Israelite spies in turn describe her "family" as "your father
and mother, your brothers and all your family [kol-bêt ʾābîk]"
(2:18). Later, in 6:23, the narrator uses the phrase "Rahab, her
father and mother and brothers and all who belonged to her"
(i.e., "her entire family," kol-mišpĕḥôtêhā), which in 6:25 is re-
phrased as "Rahab the prostitute, with her family [bêt ʾābîhā]
and all who belonged to her."

Thus, the "family" (bêt ʾāb) in ancient Canaan[4] referred to the
entire extended members of family, including male and female
servants and their families as well as resident aliens. It com-
prises "all the descendants of a single living ancestor (the head,

3. See Phyllis A. Bird, "The Harlot as Heroine: Narrative Art and Social Pre-
supposition in Three Old Testament Texts," in *Narrative Research on the Hebrew Bible*, ed. M. Amihai, G. W. Coats, and A. M. Solomon, *Semeia* 46 (1989):
120–22, 129–33.

4. See J. D. Schloen, *The House of the Father as Fact and Symbol: Patrimo-
nialism in Ugarit and the Ancient Near East*, SAHL 2 (Cambridge: Harvard
Semitic Museum, 2001), which includes (1) an analysis of households in several premodern Mediterranean societies, including Israel; (2) a survey of patrimonial society in the Bronze Age Near East, with careful criticism of
alternative models of ancient Near Eastern society; and (3) an analysis of the
role of the family in Ugarit and its mythology. This work is reviewed by
Simon B. Parker in *Religious Studies Review* 28, no. 1 (2002).

rōʾš-bêt-ʾāb) in a single lineage, excluding married daughters (who entered their husbands' *bêt-ʾāb* along with their families)."[5] An extended family or household (*bêt ʾāb*) could have had some fifty to one hundred persons, who lived in a compound dwelling unit on the inherited land.[6]

The fundamental structure of society in the historical period of ancient Israel is reflected in Josh. 7:1, where Achan is presented as "son of Carmi, the son of Zabdi, the son of Zerah, of the tribe of Judah." Here Achan son of Carmi belonged to the family of Zabdi (NIV: Zimri), who belonged to the clan (*mišpāḥâ*) of Zerah, a clan of the tribe (*maṭṭēh* [7:1, 18]; *šēbet* [7:16]) of Judah (see 7:16–18).[7] Though Achan was married and had children, he belonged to his grandfather's household. In 1 Sam. 10:20–21, however, Saul belonged to the family (*bêt ʾāb; cf.* 1 Sam. 9:20) of his father, Kish, who belonged to Matri's clan (*mišpāḥâ*),[8] a clan of the Benjaminite tribe (*šēbet*).

While a clan is referred to by the Hebrew word *mišpāḥâ*, as in 1 Sam. 20:6, where David mentions an annual sacrifice for his whole clan[9] in Bethlehem, the family as a subdivision of a clan is expressed by the phrase *bêt ʾāb* (lit., "father's house"). This can be confirmed by the phrase *kol-mišpāḥat bêt ʾābî ʾimmô*, "the whole clan of his mother's family" (NRSV, NJPS)— that is, the whole of the clan that his mother's family belonged to (lit., "the whole clan of the father's house of his mother") in Judg. 9:1 (cf. NIV: "all his mother's clan").

In some passages a woman, especially an unmarried woman, is said to have a special tie with her "mother's house" (*bêt ʾēm*). Rebekah (Gen. 24:28) and the lover's darling (Song 3:4; 8:2) seem to have belonged to their mother's living quarters while

5. Wright, "Family," 2:762.

6. See Lawrence E. Stager, "The Archaeology of the Family in Ancient Israel," *BASOR* 260 (1985): 11–24.

7. Richard S. Hess, *Joshua: An Introduction and Commentary*, TOTC (Downers Grove, Ill.: InterVarsity, 1996), 150–51.

8. Matri's name is not listed among the clans of Benjamin in Num. 26:38–41.

9. But the Hebrew term *mišpāḥâ* sometimes is used to refer to a whole people, as in Amos 3:1–2: "Hear this word the LORD has spoken against you, O people of Israel—against the whole family [*mišpāḥâ*] I brought up out of Egypt: 'You only have I chosen of all the families of the earth [*mišpĕḥôt hāʾădāmâ*]; therefore I will punish you for all your sins'" (NIV).

single, though daughters certainly were members of their extended family—that is, their "father's house." Naomi expected her two daughters-in-law to go back to their mother's living quarters, to their premarriage state (Ruth 1:8).

Sometimes, a son in a weaker and inferior position in his "father's house" would escape to his mother's relatives—that is, his mother's "brothers" (ʾăhê ʾimmô) and the "clan" of the mother's side for help (Judg. 9:1)—as with the cases of Abimelech son of Jerub-Baal, who was a son of Gideon's concubine (Judg. 8:31), and Absalom, the son of the daughter of a foreign king, who escaped to his mother's father's house after killing his brother Amnon (2 Sam. 13:34).

Joshua 7 reports that when Achan son of Carmi, the son of Zabdi, the son of Zerah, of the tribe of Judah, "coveted" (7:21) and "took" some of the devoted things, "the LORD's anger burned against Israel" (7:1 NIV). Later, in 22:20, this event is referred to as follows: "When Achan son of Zerah acted unfaithfully regarding the devoted things, did not wrath come upon the whole community of Israel? He was not the only one who died for his sin." Here, the unfaithful action of Achan, the one who belonged to the "clan" of Zerah, was regarded as that of "the whole community of Israel" (NIV).

Not only was an individual person not totally independent in the kinship structure, but also his sin was rebellion against God, who had entered into the covenant relationship with the people of Israel at Mount Sinai. As H. C. Brichto notes, "If formerly to enter a proto-Israelite family was to enter its ancestral cult and to enter its cult was to enter the family, now to enter the ʿam of YHWH was to enter the worship of YHWH and vice versa."[10] Achan thus brought God's wrath on the entire worshiping community by breaching the tenth ("Do not covet") and the eighth ("Do not steal") commandments.

Profession and Inheritance

In ancient Israel, as in other parts of the ancient Near East, it was customary for a son to follow his father's profession.

10. H. C. Brichto, "Kin, Cult, Land and Afterlife—A Biblical Complex," *HUCA* 44 (1973): 11.

Farmers' sons usually became farmers; warriors' sons became warriors, like Jesse's three sons (1 Sam. 17:13; cf. 16:18); priests' sons became priests, like Eli's sons (1 Sam. 1:3; see also 2:28; 22:20). To introduce a monarchic system into Israelite society (see 1 Sam. 8) meant that one, usually the eldest, of the king's sons was destined to become king and establish a dynasty. So it is quite understandable that Saul issued this warning and command to Jonathan, his crown prince: "As long as the son of Jesse lives on this earth, neither you nor your kingdom will be established. Now send and bring him to me, for he must die!" (1 Sam. 20:31 NIV). In this case, however, the Lord himself had rejected dynastic succession when Saul failed to obey God's commandment (see 1 Sam. 13:13–14).

Judges and prophets, however, were not hereditary in ancient Israel. Judges' sons were not judges, except for Samuel's two sons, who were appointed by their father as judges for Israel (see 1 Sam. 8:1). One might surmise that this "little dynastic experiment"[11] by Samuel, which did not wait for God himself to appoint a judge, possibly encouraged the elders of Israel to request the new institution of the monarchy, though Yahweh had ruled over his people as king from eternity (see 1 Sam. 8:5–7; also Ps. 29:10). Also, prophets were not prophets' sons, as we can see in the cases of Ezekiel the priest and Amos the cattle trader.[12]

The family (*bêt ʾāb*) was the basic unit for the system of land tenure, and each family had its own inheritance (*naḥălâ*) in the estate (land). So, if a son was not born of a normal wife, he was in a weak position in his family on the matter of inheritance. For example, though Jephthah was a mighty warrior, because his mother was not a wife of his father, Gilead, but a prostitute, the sons of Gilead's wife drove Jephthah away, saying, "You are not going to get any inheritance in our family" (Judg. 11:2).

When David spared Saul's life for the second time, he said to him, "For they have driven me out today from having a share in

11. Robert P. Gordon, *1 and 2 Samuel: A Commentary* (Exeter: Paternoster, 1986), 109.

12. When Amos said that he was neither a prophet nor a son of a prophet (Amos 7:14), the term "son" refers to a member of a prophetic guild.

the inheritance of the LORD, saying, 'Go, serve other gods!'"
(1 Sam. 26:19). Although "ancestor worship and the ultimate
ancestral ownership of the land" went together traditionally,
"in biblical religion, not the ancestors but God is the ultimate
owner of all property."[13]

Comparing "as a prince over my people Israel" (1 Sam. 9:16)
with similar wording in 1 Sam. 10:1, we see that Yahweh's "inheritance" (nahălâ, 1 Sam. 10:1) seems to refer to Yahweh's
people Israel. However, the primary meaning of the term is "in-
alienable, hereditary property."[14] Both "land" and "heir" are the
two items of the divine promise to Abraham (see, e.g., Gen.
12:7), and these two terms appear as a word pair in passages
such as Deut. 9:26–29; Isa. 19:25; Joel 2:17; Ps. 78:71; 94:5. The
"land" of Israel was won in the conquest, granted by God to the
individuals, then passed down by inheritance. So Yahweh's "inheritance" (nahălâ) refers not only to the land but also to his
people.

The land belonged to the family, so it could not be sold per-
manently to those outside of the family. This principle of in-
alienability is well illustrated in the story of Naboth's vineyard
in 1 Kings 21. When Naboth was offered better land or good
payment in exchange for his vineyard next to Ahab's palace, he
rejected this offer, saying, "The LORD forbid that I should give
you the inheritance of my fathers" (1 Kings 21:3 NIV). If someone sold land to a fellow Israelite for some reason, the law set
the institution of the Jubilee, in which "each one of you is to return to his family property and each to his own clan" (Lev.
25:10 NIV). In this way, one could "maintain the viability of families on their own land by periodic restoration. It illustrates the
point that Israel's economic system was geared—in principle at
least, if not in practice—not to the interests of a wealthy elite,
but to the economic survival and social health of the lowest socioeconomic units: the extended families on their patrimonial
land."[15]

13. Brichto, "Kin, Cult, Land and Afterlife," 11.
14. *HALOT*, 687.
15. Wright, "Family," 2:764.

Fathers' Roles: Patriarchy

As the head of a family, the father had legal authority and responsibility over the family members in various aspects of life. In turn, children were supposed to obey and honor their parents so that they might live long in the land that Yahweh granted them (Exod. 20:12). The father was responsible for disciplining his sons and daughters and approving their marriages and professions. Samson's parents gave their approval to their son marrying a Philistine woman, though reluctantly (Judg. 14:3). When Saul wanted David to serve him, he sent a messenger asking his father, and Jesse permitted his son to go and then sent gifts to the king (1 Sam. 16:17–20). The head of the family was also one of the elders of the community and engaged in local civic matters at the city gate. When Boaz wanted a legal settlement with regard to Ruth, he dealt with his relative at the gate before ten elders (Ruth 4:1–2).

Besides teaching God's law to his children (see Deut. 6:7; 11:19), the father was to explain to them about God's work in the history of the covenant people. For example, Joshua asked the people to take twelve stones from the middle of the Jordan to serve as a sign. Later, when people asked their fathers, "What do these stones mean?" (Josh. 4:6, 21), the head of the family was to "tell them that the flow of the Jordan was cut off before the ark of the covenant of the LORD. When it crossed the Jordan, the waters of the Jordan were cut off" (Josh. 4:7 NIV; also 4:23). Therefore, the stones were to be "a memorial to the people of Israel forever" (4:7 NIV). These stones were visual aids to teach the future generations about God's work at the Jordan.

Sometimes the responsibility of being the head of the family was assumed by the eldest son. Such a system of "fratriarchy"[16] can be seen in the case in which Laban acted as the head of family with regard to the marriage of his sister Rebekah in Gen. 24. It was only after Abraham's servant explained the whole story about why he came to Aram-Naharaim that Rebekah's father, Bethuel, appears (see 24:47). Even then he is mentioned after

16. C. H. Gordon, "Fratriarchy in the Old Testament," *JBL* 54 (1935): 223–31; C. H. Gordon and G. A. Rendsburg, *The Bible and the Ancient Near East,* 4th ed. (New York: Norton, 1997), 121.

his son: "Laban and Bethuel" (24:50). When the father reached old age, he could entrust his authority to his eldest son to act as fratriarch while he was still alive.

The same custom seems to have been practiced in Jesse's family. David hints that his brother, as a fratriarch, could order him to be at the "annual sacrifice . . . for his whole clan [*mišpāḥâ*]" in 1 Sam. 20:6, 29. This is quite possible because his father, Jesse, had already retired because of his old age.[17]

Redeemer: *Gōʾēl* (the Nearest Kin)

In the family system of ancient Israel, the nearest relative was supposed to redeem, or buy back, a family estate (land) that had been taken into the hand of the outsider because of poverty (Lev. 25:25). Another important duty was to raise a male heir for a deceased relative by marrying the childless widow.[18] According to Deut. 25:5–6,

> If brothers are living together and one of them dies without a son, his widow must not marry outside the family. Her husband's brother shall take her and marry her and fulfill the duty of a brother-in-law to her. The first son she bears shall carry on the name of the dead brother so that his name will not be blotted out from Israel. (NIV)

This system is known as "levirate marriage," from Latin *levir,* which means "brother-in-law" (see Matt. 22:24; Mark 12:19). When Naomi told her two daughters-in-law to return to their premarriage state (Ruth 1:12–13), she said,

> Return home, my daughters; I am too old to have another husband. Even if I thought there was still hope for me—even if I had a husband tonight and then gave birth to sons—would you wait until they grew up? Would you remain unmarried for them? No,

17. Jesse became "a senior citizen." See 1 Sam. 17:12, where Jesse is said to have "become a senior" (*bāʾ baʾănāšîm*; lit., "came into men")—that is, he had reached the age where he was exempted from civil and military services.

18. See Robert L. Hubbard Jr., *The Book of Ruth,* NICOT (Grand Rapids: Eerdmans, 1988), 56–62, 188–89.

my daughters. It is more bitter for me than for you, because the
Lord's hand has gone out against me! (NIV)

Was she referring to the institution of levirate marriage here?
Probably. But unfortunately, there were no brothers-in-law for
her widowed daughters-in-law, Ruth and Orpah.[19]

When Naomi wanted to sell the estate of her husband,
Elimelech, Boaz asked the nearest relative, who had the right to
redeem the land, if he was willing to do so. If he was, he should
also "acquire the dead man's widow [= Ruth], in order to maintain the name of the dead with his property" (Ruth 4:5 NIV).
When this *gōʾēl*, "kinsman-redeemer" (NIV; cf. NRSV: "the next-of-
kin"), was informed of this obligation, he gave up his right of
redemption (4:6). So Boaz, the next to him, redeemed Elimelech's estate and acquired Ruth, the childless widow of Naomi's
son. Thus Ruth became Boaz's wife and gave birth to Obed, the
grandfather of David (4:9–22). Living in a totally different culture, we are not called to follow Boaz's example literally, but we
should show our concern and compassion toward our own
family members who are in need of our help.

Marriage

Though the purpose of levirate marriage was "to maintain
the name of the dead with his property," the original intention
of the institution of marriage in the Bible was not only for procreation but also for companionship and mutual support. Genesis 2:24 and the common prophetic imagery of Israel's exclusive relationship with Yahweh being that of the sole wife to the
divine husband shows that monogamy was the ideal. Song of
Songs naturally assumes that the loving relationship between
the lover and the beloved is exclusive of any other persons.

However, when procreation became the major purpose for
marriage in the society of extended families, it was customary
for a wealthy person to take another wife to produce an heir in
case the first wife was barren. This situation led Elkanah to take

19. K. Nielsen, *Ruth: A Commentary*, OTL (Louisville: Westminster John
Knox, 1997), 47–48.

a second wife, Peninnah, besides Hannah, the barren wife. Such polygamy may have provided heirs, but it also caused tensions among the family, especially between the two wives (1 Sam. 1:6–7). This rivalry escalated when the husband loved the childless wife more than the mother of his heirs (see 1:5, 8). It is impossible for a man to truly love more than one woman at the same time without favoritism, for exclusiveness is the nature of love between husband and wife. God created a woman for the man as a helpmate, "bone of my bones and flesh of my flesh" (Gen. 2:23).

Religious harmony is always very important for a good marriage, for it is only when husband and wife stand before the same God that they love and trust each other. So marriage with foreigners is prohibited in the law, which "disapproved of it (at least, as regards the Canaanite population, Deut. 7:3[–4]) and in post-exilic times draconian measures were taken against foreign marriages by Ezra (Ezra 9 and 10) and Nehemiah (Neh. 10:30; 13:23–37)."[20] Although we aren't told why, Naomi's sons married Moabite women. Yet one of them, Ruth, followed Naomi, her mother-in-law, regarded Naomi's God as her own God, and served her and her God faithfully: "But Ruth replied, 'Don't urge me to leave you or to turn back from you. Where you go I will go, and where you stay I will stay. Your people will be my people and your God my God'" (Ruth 1:16 NIV).[21]

However, Solomon's marriages with Pharaoh's daughter (1 Kings 3:1) and with numerous foreign women (1 Kings 11:1–3) were political ones. These wives "led him astray" and "turned his heart after other gods" (11:4), such as "Ashtoreth the goddess of the Sidonians, and Molech the detestable god of the Ammonites" (11:5 NIV) as well as "Chemosh the detestable god of Moab" (11:7 NIV).

> They were from nations about which the LORD had told the Israelites, "You must not intermarry with them, because they will surely turn your hearts after their gods." Nevertheless, Solomon held fast to them in love. (1 Kings 11:2 NIV)

20. Wright, "Family," 2:766.
21. On this verse, see Hubbard, *Book of Ruth*, 117–18.

Later, Ahab "married Jezebel daughter of Ethbaal king of the Sidonians, and began to serve Baal and worship him" (1 Kings 16:31 NIV). While Ruth and her husband had the same religion, honoring one and the same God, Solomon and Ahab married women from different religions and strayed from trusting the Lord. For a member of the worshiping community of Yahweh, nothing, not even marriage, should interfere with this covenant relationship with him.

The Problem of Childlessness

In ancient Israel children were regarded as a precious gift from God (e.g., Ps. 127:3; 128:3). Barrenness or loss of children was considered a great tragedy. Intentional abortion is mentioned neither in the Bible nor in the texts of the West Semitic world. Accidental "abortion" (i.e., miscarriage) was much feared. It was customary that a pregnant woman stayed home quietly for the first five months[22] until the pregnancy became stable and without fear of miscarriage (see Luke 1:24; *KTU* 1.23.56–57 [*UT* 52.56–57]).[23]

Childbirth was a happy time for parents, and either father or mother named the child. Samson (Judg. 13:24) and Ichabod (1 Sam. 4:21) were named by their mothers, but Solomon was named by his father, David (2 Sam. 12:24 [*Kethib*, the traditional consonants]; cf. "she named" [*Qere*, as later vocalized]); his other name, Jedidiah, was given by the Lord (12:24–25).

For any family, no heir meant the cessation of the "house"; for a king, the cessation of his dynasty.[24] Because Absalom had no son to carry on the memory of his name, he erected a pillar in the King's Valley as "a monument to himself" and named it "after himself" (2 Sam. 18:18). Death of the sons (heirs) in one's old age or widowhood led to a desperate situation because the old couple (like Abraham and Sarah; see also 2 Kings 4:14) or a

22. Based on the lunar calendar.

23. D. T. Tsumura, "A Problem of Myth and Ritual Relationship: *CTA* 23 (*UT* 52): 56–57 Reconsidered," *UF* 10 (1978): 387–95.

24. D. T. Tsumura, "The Problem of Childlessness in the Royal Epic of Ugarit," in *Monarchies and Socio-Religious Traditions in the Ancient Near East*, ed. T. Mikasa (Wiesbaden: Harrassowitz, 1984), 11–20.

widow (like Naomi, Ruth's mother-in-law, and like the widow during Elijah's time in 1 Kings 17:17) would have no chance to get another son.

God through special grace gave a son to an aged couple such as Abraham and Sarah and to barren and sterile wives such as Samson's mother (Judg. 13:2), Samuel's mother (Hannah; 1 Sam. 1), and the wealthy Shunammite woman (2 Kings 4:16a). Hannah acknowledges in her prayer (1 Sam. 2:5b), "She who was barren has borne seven children, but she who has had many sons pines away" (NIV). It is by God's sovereign will that a barren woman would bear "seven children."[25] Considering that the barrenness was viewed as tragedy and disgrace, how happy these women were when they bore a son!

On the other hand, losing a son was an extremely sad experience. In Naomi's case, she became a widow and lost both of her sons (Ruth 1:3–5), leaving her completely without an heir. Two deaths—the death of a husband and the death of a son(s)—have been depicted by the two weapons of the god/angel of death in ancient Canaan. For example, the god *Mot-wa-Shar* ("Death-and-Evil") in an Ugaritic ritual text (*KTU* 1.23.8–9 [*UT* 52.8–9]) holds two staffs: the staff of privation (*ht ṭkl*) and the staff of bereavement (*ht ulmn*). This is also represented in one Aramaic magic bowl, in both text and picture, as the angel of death holding two weapons of death.[26] Exactly the same two key words, *ʾlmn* and *škl*, appear in Isa. 47:8–9. Privation of an only son certainly was a tragic experience for a widow. When Jesus saw a widow's only son being carried dead at Nain, he was deeply moved by this sad event ("had compassion for her" [NRSV]; "his heart went out to her" [NIV]) and raised him from the dead (Luke 7:11–15).

Orphans and Widows

In the ancient Near East, those without the head of the family (e.g., an orphan without a father or a widow without a hus-

25. For the theme of an ideal woman having "seven sons," see Ruth 4:15; Job 1:2; 42:13; Jer. 15:9; Acts 19:14; Keret Epic, *KTU* 1.15.II.23 (*UT* 128.II.23). See also *CAD*, H (1956), 200 on AMA 7, "a mother of seven (children)."

26. D. T. Tsumura, "A Ugaritic God, *Mt-w-Šr*, and His Two Weapons (*UT* 52:8–11)," *UF* 6 (1974): 407–13.

band) were to be protected by kings. In the Ugaritic royal epics, King Dani'il is described to have sat at the entrance of the city gate and "judged the widow's case, made decisions regarding the orphan" (*KTU* 1.17.V.7–8).[27] King Keret is accused by his son during his illness as follows:

> You do not judge the widow's case,
> you do not make a decision regarding the oppressed. . . .
> Before you, you do not feed the orphan,
> behind your back the widow. (*KTU* 1.16.VI.33–34, 49–50)[28]

The biblical law also commands the people not to "abuse" (NRSV) or "take advantage of" (NIV) a widow or an orphan (Exod. 22:22). The Lord warns,

> If you do and they cry out to me, I will certainly hear their cry.
> My anger will be aroused, and I will kill you with the sword;
> your wives will become widows and your children fatherless.
>   (Exod. 22:23–24 NIV)

So, the Lord is the one "who executes justice for the orphan and the widow, and who loves the strangers, providing them food and clothing" (Deut. 10:18 NRSV). A command comes: "You shall also love the stranger, for you were strangers in the land of Egypt" (Deut. 10:19 NRSV). Such commandments were given to the covenant people as a whole, not just to the leaders or kings. The Lord also commands the people through the prophet Isaiah (Isa. 1:17), "Seek justice, encourage the oppressed. Defend the cause of the fatherless, plead the case of the widow" (NIV).

His commandment thus is very practical:

> When you reap your harvest in your field and forget a sheaf in the field, you shall not go back to get it; it shall be left for the alien, the orphan, and the widow, so that the LORD your God may bless you in all your undertakings. (Deut. 24:19 NRSV)

27. D. Pardee, "The 'Aqhatu Legend," in *The Context of Scripture*, vol. 1, *Canonical Compositions from the Biblical World*, ed. W. W. Hallo and K. L. Younger Jr. (Leiden: Brill, 1997), 346.

28. D. Pardee, "The Kirta Epic," in Hallo and Younger, eds., *Canonical Compositions*, 342.

Even during the time when "everyone did what was right in his own eyes" (Judg. 17:6; 21:25), this legal tradition was alive, and people in Israelite society practiced this welfare toward the needy. Naomi and Ruth, both widows, obtained their food from the harvest field, collecting sheaves that were left (Ruth 2:2–7). In New Testament times, this biblical principle was carried on by the church. Paul advises Timothy to "give proper recognition to those widows who are really in need" (1 Tim. 5:3 NIV; also 5:5, 16). The community of believers must provide "homes" for the homeless and "families" for orphans and widows, both spiritually and materially.

Parental Authority

Parental authority was particularly strong in ancient Israel. The duty of children to honor and obey their parents is stressed throughout the Old Testament (e.g., Exod. 20:12; 21:15, 17; Deut. 21:18–21; 27:16; Proverbs in various places). In Judg. 19:24, as in Gen. 19:8, a father is described to have had the authority even to sacrifice his daughter's virginity. Also, Jephthah is said to have sacrificed his daughter's life to fulfill his vow to the Lord (Judg. 11:30–31, 39; cf. Gen. 22:2). However, these examples do not mean that fathers normally had the freedom to control their children's life and death, even though children were considered part of the father's property. An evil son could be put to death only if both parents took him to court, and then the whole community killed him (Deut. 21:18–21). It is certainly only God who has authority over human life and death, as Hannah expresses in her "prayer" in 1 Sam. 2:6. And indeed, as a psalmist declares, "Sons are a heritage from the Lord, children a reward from him" (Ps. 127:3 NIV).

The child sacrifice practiced in the northern kingdom before the destruction of Samaria (see 2 Kings 17:17) and in Jerusalem during the reign of Ahaz (16:3) and Manasseh (21:6) was a pagan religious practice introduced to the covenant people. In official Yahwism this was clearly rejected as an abominable action against the covenant God.

The Father-Son Relationship

In various places, the Book of Proverbs stresses the importance of obedience to parents' admonitions (Prov. 1:8; 6:20; cf. Eph. 6:1). However, the father-son relationship in ancient Israel was in reality far from being ideal. In the Historical Books, we see examples of great leaders who were not good fathers, yet their negative experiences have a great deal of educational significance as "cautionary examples" to us.

Eli and Samuel and Their Sons

The old priest Eli could not control his two evil sons. They treated the Lord's offering with contempt (1 Sam. 2:17) and "slept with the women who served at the entrance to the Tent of Meeting" (2:22 NIV). Eli's inability to manage his own sons as a father and a senior priest was condemned by the Lord: "Why do you scorn my sacrifice and offering that I prescribed for my dwelling? Why do you honor your sons more than me by fattening yourselves on the choice parts of every offering made by my people Israel?" (2:29 NIV). Therefore, not only did the Lord judge Eli's two sons, Hophni and Phinehas, by putting them to death "on the same day" (see 2:34; 4:11, 17), but also Eli's family (bêt, lit., "house") was punished forever "because of the sin he knew about; his sons made themselves contemptible, and he failed to restrain them" (3:13 NIV).

When Samuel became old, he appointed his own sons, Joel and Abijah, "as judges for Israel" at Beersheba (8:1–2 NIV). Though Samuel himself walked with integrity until his death (see 12:3–5), his sons with their good religious names "turned aside after dishonest gain and accepted bribes and perverted justice" (8:3 NIV). One might wonder whether Samuel acted responsibly in choosing his own sons as judges, for until now the Lord had raised judges as the crises came. Samuel's appointment of his own sons as his successors possibly showed a lack of faith that God would send a "savior" in due course (see Judg. 3:9 [Othniel], 15 [Ehud], 31 [Shamgar], and so on). What is certain is that Samuel in his old age failed to train his sons to walk in his steps.

Saul and Jonathan

In contrast, Saul seemed to have had a good relationship with his father, Kish, and normally with his son Jonathan. Saul was "an impressive young man without equal among the Israelites" (1 Sam. 9:2 NIV). When Kish asked Saul to search for some lost donkeys, he went out with his servant. When the search took longer than he expected, Saul was concerned that his father might be worrying about him (9:5), while Kish, on his part, was asking, "What shall I do about my son?" (10:2). Here is a beautiful relationship between father and son, each thinking of the other.

Jonathan also was a model son to his father, Saul. As the eldest son, Jonathan helped his father in fighting against the Philistines. Saul entrusted one-third of his army to his son's hand; thus, father and son worked together against the enemy encamped at Michmash (1 Sam. 13:2). When Saul, his father, became David's enemy, Jonathan still managed to keep a fairly good relationship with his father. In the earlier stage, Saul told Jonathan of his intention to kill David, but he also listened to Jonathan's advice and even took an oath not to kill David (19:1, 6). Even after David fled from Saul to save his life, Jonathan still took his relation to his father positively, saying, "Look, my father doesn't do anything, great or small, without confiding in me. Why would he hide this from me? It's not so!" (20:2 NIV; cf. 20:12). Is this Jonathan's naïveté?[29] Possibly. Taking his complete trust in the Lord in 14:6 ("Perhaps the LORD will act in our behalf. Nothing can hinder the LORD from saving, whether by many or by few" [NIV]), Jonathan was not simply a naïve person. When he realized that his father really intended to kill David, "Jonathan got up from the table in fierce anger; on that second day of the month he did not eat, because he was grieved at his father's shameful treatment of David" (20:34 NIV). By this time, Saul was insane and could not judge the situation reasonably, overreacting against his son Jonathan: "My son has incited my servant to lie in wait for me, as he does today" (22:8 NIV). Despite his father's unreasonable treatment of his friend, Jonathan

29. David Gunn sees Jonathan's speech as being full of irony and naïveté. See Gunn's, *The Fate of King Saul*, JSOTSup 14 (Sheffield: JSOT Press, 1980), 84.

stayed faithful to his father, even fighting with him against the Philistines and dying with him on Mount Gilboa.

Jesse and David

David was the youngest son of Jesse at Bethlehem, shepherding his father's sheep (1 Sam. 16:11). His three oldest brothers were on the battlefield with Saul, and the eldest brother, Eliab, probably assumed authority as a fratriarch (17:28; 20:29). When David fled from Saul and escaped to the cave of Adullam, "his brothers and his father's household [*ʾeḥāyw wěkol-bêt ʾābîw*] . . . went down to him there" (22:1 NIV). Though the youngest, David now acted as a fratriarch; he assumed responsibility for his elderly parents by taking them over to the Moabite king at Mizpah and asking him to shelter them (22:3). One can only imagine how hard it was for the elderly persons to go down to the Dead Sea (four hundred meters below sea level) and back up to almost the same height above sea level (more than three hundred meters) to Mizpah of Moab. David showed a special concern to spare his parents from having to share his unstable and dangerous life.

David and His Sons

In contrast, the relationship between David and his sons in the second half of his life, especially after he became involved in adultery with Bathsheba, had many problems. David certainly had to harvest the fruits of his sinful conduct in his family. When David heard that his firstborn son, Amnon, had raped Tamar, the sister of Absalom, his third son (see 2 Sam. 3:2–3), he was very angry (2 Sam. 13:21), but it seems that he did not do anything further about the matter (see 2 Sam. 14). The narrator says, "Absalom never said a word to Amnon, either good or bad; he hated Amnon because he had disgraced his sister Tamar" (13:22 NIV).

So, Absalom's hatred grew and matured, and finally, after two years of premeditation, he killed Amnon and fled to his mother's father, the king of Geshur (13:34, 37). Absalom, the son of a foreign king's daughter and, hence, one in a weaker position among his brothers, became higher in rank toward the royal throne because David's first son, Amnon, the son of Ahinoam of Jezreel, died. David's second son, Kileab, the son of Abigail, apparently died early, as there is no mention of him in the narratives. David could have anticipated such an internal struggle among his sons and prevented this tragedy beforehand, but he did not do anything. After it happened, David simply "mourned for his son every day" (13:37 NIV).

In monogamy, with the help of his wife, a troubled father could have done something to deal with "sibling rivalry." But with two different mothers involved, the rivalry between two sons could be more severe. "Although there is no direct evidence for the way in which multiple wives shared responsibilities of household management . . . , some form of seniority system may be assumed, especially where a second wife had the status of a concubine. Each woman, however, would have control over her own children."[30] A father of many sons and husband of many wives probably would prefer to step out of domestic struggles. So David did nothing to solve this situation. Having more than one wife certainly caused more trouble than happiness in the family. A British missionary to Japan once said, "The best way to educate your children is to love their mother."

Even though Absalom came back to Jerusalem, David did not let him see his face for two years (14:24, 28). When he finally summoned him, "he came in and bowed down with his face to the ground before the king. And the king kissed Absalom" (14:33 NIV). But this seemingly was not a real reconciliation between father and son. Finally, Absalom rebelled against his own father. King David escaped, going out of Jerusalem barefoot as he wept (15:30). However, David showed special concern for Absalom even when he was an enemy who was seeking his own life, and he commanded his men to "protect" Absalom for his own sake (18:12). David's ambivalence thus gave his men a strong sense of betrayal. When David was informed of the death of Absalom, he wept, mourning for Absalom, "O my son Absalom! My son, my son Absalom! If only I had died instead of you—O Absalom, my

30. Phyllis A. Bird, "Women: Old Testament," ABD 6:954.

son, my son!" (18:33 NIV). And thus, because of David's grief, "for the whole army the victory that day was turned into mourning" (19:2 NIV). Because of his blind affection and mixed emotions toward his son, David lacked determination and leadership not only in domestic affairs but also in this national crisis.

David's fourth son, Adonijah, born next after Absalom (2 Sam. 3:4; 1 Kings 1:6), exalted himself, saying, "I will be king" (1 Kings 1:5). He is said to have been "very handsome," and David had never "scolded" (NJPS) him by asking, "Why do you behave as you do?" (1:6 NIV). David here again failed to raise his children to fear the Lord and honor their father and mother. David might have had hesitation about disciplining his son firmly because he feared that he might lose another son. At the same time, David had sworn to Bathsheba that her son Solomon should be his successor (1:17, 20). David's indeterminate attitudes caused these unnecessary tragedies in his family. Usually, though not always, a father should act firmly toward his son, while accepting him as an independent person with love.

Death, Mourning, and Burial

Death was a major concern in a family. When Samuel died, all the Israelites "assembled and mourned for him" and buried him at his home (*bêtô*; lit., "his house") in Ramah (1 Sam. 25:1 NIV; also 28:3a). Barzillai expressed his desire to die and be buried in his hometown "near the tomb of [his] father and mother" (2 Sam. 19:37). David brought the bones of Saul and his son Jonathan back from Jabesh Gilead and buried them "in the tomb of Saul's father Kish, at Zela in Benjamin" (2 Sam. 21:11– 14 NIV). And David himself "rested with his fathers and was buried in the City of David" (1 Kings 2:10 NIV). Thus, care for the dead through burial was a very important part of family life in ancient Israel.

However, the people did not worship the dead ancestor as a divine being, as did other peoples in Canaan. In the Ugaritic story of Aqhat, it is stated that one of the duties of the son, normally the eldest one, was to set up "the stela of the divine ancestor"[31] for his family in the shrine (see, e.g., *KTU* 1.17.I.26). However, no such obligation was put on a son in ancient Israel, for ancestor worship was not practiced there, at least on the official level. There is no sign that Israelites worshiped even David. Certainly, worshiping the spirits of the dead was an abomination to the Lord God.[32]

Conclusions: Implications for Today's Society

In our world of cultural relativism, it seems that there exist no absolute principles in family relationships and life ethics. However, biblical principles and the basic needs of the family remain the same, though the cultural settings in the Historical Books of the Old Testament are quite different from our postmodern society, in which humans frequently play God by interfering in the mystery of human life by abortion, cloning, and euthanasia.

Examples in the lives of Joshua, Ruth, Elkanah, Hannah, Samuel, Saul, David, and others urge us to reconsider the significance of the Ten Commandments. Are not abortion and euthanasia breaches of the sixth commandment ("Do not kill")? We should ask ourselves if parents have a right to abuse their own children, if a child is the possession of the parents, and if marriage can be ended freely by the consent of husband and wife. Have tenderness toward the weak and disabled as well as respect toward the elderly been nurtured first in our family? Does honoring parents (the fifth commandment) remain the basic condition for a happy family life? Should society show more concern toward the homeless and toward orphans and

31. See J. F. Healey, "Ilib," in *DDD*, 436–48; K. van der Toorn, "Ilib and the 'God of the Father,'" *UF* 25 (1993): 379–87; D. T. Tsumura, "The Interpretation of the Ugaritic Funerary Text *KTU* 1.161," in *Official Cult and Popular Religion in the Ancient Near East*, ed. E. Matsushima (Heidelberg: Winter, 1993), 48; idem, "Kings and Cults in Ancient Ugarit," in *Priests and Officials in the Ancient Near East*, ed. K. Watanabe (Heidelberg: Winter, 1999), 222–23. Cf. Pardee, "'Aqhatu Legend," 1:344 n. 6, which takes it as "the god of the father."

32. For Canaanite practices of ancestor worship, or cult of the dead, see T. J. Lewis, *Cults of the Dead in Ancient Israel and Ugarit*, HSM 39 (Atlanta: Scholars Press, 1989).

widows? Should the church as a believing and worshiping community provide a home for the needy?

The biblical concept of family is more than a physical and cultural one; it is a spiritual community in the Redeemer. God's family includes both earthly family and heavenly family. The very basic principle in the Bible is still this: even if other people choose to serve other gods, "as for me and my household, we will serve the LORD."

4

Family in the Wisdom Literature

TREMPER LONGMAN III

What is Wisdom literature? To answer this question, we must begin with another: What is wisdom? These questions draw us almost immediately to the Book of Proverbs.

We know Proverbs as a book that presents observations, advice, warnings, and guidance on how to live life. Life is filled with obstacles and difficulties, and the Book of Proverbs helps its readers know how to navigate life on ground level. It is often rightly said that biblical wisdom is skill rather than intellectual knowledge pure and simple. Wisdom is strikingly similar to what has been called "emotional intelligence,"[1] which should be contrasted with intelligence. People with a high I.Q. know many facts; they can solve difficult mathematical equations. Their ability to reason and use logic is superior to others. On the other hand, a person with emotional intelligence has other skills, which include such characteristics as "self-control, zeal and persistence and the ability to motivate oneself."[2] Emotional intelligence also includes "abilities such as being able to motivate oneself and persist in the face of frustration; to control im-

1. See D. Goleman, *Emotional Intelligence* (New York: Bantam, 1995).
2. Ibid., xii.

pulse and delay gratification; to regulate one's mood and keep distress from swamping the ability to think; to empathize and to hope."[3] Interestingly, studies have shown that it is emotional intelligence and not I.Q. that correlates with success in life— that is, the ability to get and hold a good job, enjoy life, and sustain healthy relationships.

Biblical wisdom, then, is much closer to emotional intelligence than it is to I.Q. Biblical wisdom is, in large part at least, skill in living in the midst of the turmoil of life. As we read Proverbs, we see wisdom demonstrated in a wide variety of life circumstances. We learn about wealth and poverty, productive and destructive speech, relationships with friends and neighbors, pride and humility, to name just a few of the topics treated. Our description of biblical wisdom encourages us to think that the book may say something about the family and family relationships, and in this we are not disappointed. Indeed, Proverbs has much to say about the family and, arguably, derives from a family context.

However, before plunging into the book's observations and instructions about the family, we must come to a better understanding of its genre, structure, and overall message.[4] The book's macrostructure contains two parts. Proverbs 1–9 contains extended discourses, while the remainder of the book is composed of the short, pithy statements that we usually associate with the term "proverb." Later, we will see how Prov. 1–9 casts its long shadow on the second part of the book. But our more immediate concern is to come to grips with the genre of the proverbial saying. After all, genre triggers reading strategy.[5] So what is a proverb and how does it function?

A proverb is a poetical form that expresses an insight, an observation, or advice that has been popularly accepted as a gen-

3. Ibid., 34.
4. For a fuller discussion, see R. B. Dillard and T. Longman III, *Introduction to the Old Testament* (Grand Rapids: Zondervan, 1994), 235–45; T. Longman III, *How to Read Proverbs* (Downers Grove, Ill.: InterVarsity, 2002).
5. See my comments on genre in T. Longman III, "Form Criticism, Recent Developments in Genre Theory, and the Evangelical," *WTJ* 47 (1985): 46–67; idem, *Literary Approaches to Biblical Interpretation* (Grand Rapids: Zondervan, 1987), 76–83.

eral truth. Indeed, a proverb has been so universally accepted as expressing something true that all it takes to end a discussion is to cite it at the appropriate time.

Be careful to notice that a proverb is accepted as true only if applied at the right time.[6] This is a characteristic of proverbs of any culture. Indeed, proverbs that seem contradictory when listed out of a social context may make perfect sense if used in the right circumstance. My grandmother, who loved to cook alone, would announce to my mother, "Too many cooks spoil the broth," but when the dishes were ready to be washed, she would state with equal vehemence, "Many hands make light work."

The Book of Proverbs recognizes the circumstantial truth of its sayings. After all, it is "timely advice" that is lovely and compared to "golden apples in a silver basket" (Prov. 25:11). Cheerful songs may encourage people at the right time, but according to Prov. 25:20,

> Singing songs to a person with a heavy heart
> is like taking someone's jacket in cold weather
> or rubbing salt in a wound.

We can see the importance of this understanding of the genre before we actually explore the teaching of Proverbs on the family. Much of what it presents is not law; it contains principles that are generally true depending on the people involved, the time, as well as more general circumstances. Memorizing proverbs and applying them mechanically to every and any situation is useless ("A proverb in the mouth of a fool is as useless as a paralyzed leg" [Prov. 26:7]), even harmful ("A proverb in the mouth of a fool is like a thornbush brandished by a drunk" [Prov. 26:9]).

This understanding of the genre of proverb makes sense of the so-called contradictory proverbs. The most famous of these is the pair that concerns whether or not to answer a fool.

> Do not answer a fool according to his folly,
> or you will be like him yourself.

6. B. Kirschenblatt-Gimblett, "Toward a Theory of Proverb Meaning," *Proverbium* 22 (1973): 821–27; C. Fontaine, "Proverb Performance in the Hebrew Bible," *JSOT* 32 (1985): 87–103.

> Answer a fool according to his folly,
>   or he will be wise in his own eyes. (Prov. 26:4–5 NIV)

These two proverbs are side by side, and the wise know which one to apply in a certain situation.

With this introduction, let us now turn our attention to the passages that help us reconstruct the book's understanding and advice concerning the family. I begin with five principles that are relevant to the family in general and the parent-child relationship in particular and then continue with five instructions that shape the bond between husbands and wives.

Family in General and the Parent-Child Relationship in Particular

1. *The Book of Proverbs insists on the importance of a strong, cohesive family. It denigrates anyone and anything that erodes the family bond.*

> There are six things the LORD hates—
>   no, seven things he detests:
> haughty eyes,
> a lying tongue,
> hands that kill the innocent,
> a heart that plots evil,
> feet that race to do wrong,
> a false witness who pours out lies,
> a person who sows discord in a family. (Prov. 6:16–19)

This numerical parallelism lists character traits that lead to social fragmentation. Many scholars think that the climax is the seventh and final colon, which points to fragmentation in the family (cf. "Those who trouble their families inherit the wind" [11:29a]).

Individuals flourish best in a family context. Proverbs 27:8 implies this when it compares a person who leaves home to a bird who strays from the nest. A bird away from the nest is prey to predators and may not find enough food to survive.

The suggestion is that it is foolhardy to leave the protective family context.

However, cohesive families do not happen naturally, and Proverbs presents many admonitions to build up the family:

> A wise woman builds her home,
>> but a foolish woman tears it down with her own hands.
>> (14:1)

2. *In the Book of Proverbs, instruction takes place in a family setting.* Where the teacher and the pupil are identified in Proverbs, it is usually, but not always, a father who addresses a son. As is well known, one of the issues in the interpretation of Proverbs is whether this father-son relationship is better understood as teacher-pupil or master-apprentice. This debate is associated with the question of whether the setting of Proverbs is the school or the family.[7] On the latter question, I agree with Fox that there likely were schools during at least some of the Old Testament period, even though we do not have explicit evidence of schools until the Hellenistic period. But even if there were schools, and even if proverbs were part of a school's curriculum, that does not demand that the origin or even the exclusive use of proverbs be located in that setting.

In my opinion, there is little doubt that the Book of Proverbs intends for us to understand the father-son relationship in Proverbs, particularly chapters 1–9, as a biological relationship. Most telling is the mention of the mother in 1:8, 6:20, and 31:1. Though she never speaks, it is clear that the father often speaks on behalf of both parents as he instructs the son.

In addition, the father speaks not only his wisdom but also the wisdom of the generations. His father instructed him, and now he is passing on this familial wisdom to the next generation. This is clear in the words of 4:3–4:

> For I, too, was once my father's son,
>> tenderly loved as my mother's only child.
> My father taught me. . . .

---

7. For an important discussion and relevant bibliography, see M. V. Fox, *Proverbs 1–9*, AB 18A (Garden City, N.Y.: Doubleday, 2000), 6–12.

I do not mean this to imply that all the proverbs in the book
have a familial setting, as some are clearly connected to the
court, but this should not make us lose sight of the fact that
most of the wisdom instruction takes place between a biological parent and a child.[8]

3. *Children must respect the teaching of their parents.* Some of
the most extensive teaching in the second part of Proverbs has
to do with this topic. The list is quite long,[9] so here I present
three passages that are representative.

> If you insult your father or mother,
>> the lamp of your life will be snuffed out. (20:20)

> Some people curse their father
>> and do not thank their mother.
> They are pure in their own eyes,
>> but they are filthy and unwashed.
> They look proudly around,
>> casting disdainful glances.
> They have teeth like swords
>> and fangs like knives.
> They devour the poor from the earth
>> and the needy from among humanity. (30:11–14)

But perhaps the hardest-hitting proverb in this vein is 30:17:

> The eye that mocks the father
>> and despises a mother's instructions
> Will be plucked out by ravens of the valley
>> and eaten by vultures.

8. I believe that this position holds even if the final redaction of the Book of
Proverbs is the work of sages connected with the court or temple. They would
have collected and preserved wisdom sayings that derived from family settings
and that were intended to be used in a family setting. Also, I think that the content of Proverbs indicates a variety of socioeconomic backgrounds to individual proverbs. Some proverbs clearly emanate from, and find their primary use
in, a modest farming village, while others make sense only in the highest levels
of the society.

9. Besides those quoted here, see 10:1; 13:1; 15:5, 20; 17:21, 25; 19:26; 28:7,
24; 29:3. Some of these proverbs speak of the shame that disrespectful children
bring on their parents.

These proverbs make it quite clear that the child must follow the parents' instructions. At this point it is helpful to issue a reminder, especially as we begin to think of contemporary application of this material to our own lives: proverbs are not law, but rather, generally true principles that are dependent on time and circumstances. The Book of Proverbs is not teaching that all children must obey their parents' instruction without hesitation. The preunderstanding of these proverbs is that the parents themselves are godly and righteous and that their instruction reflects wisdom. A foolish parent should not be obeyed, and it is a travesty to use proverbs to support an uncritical obedience to even godly parents.

Perhaps this is as good a place as any to raise the issue of the "son" (*bēn*) in the Book of Proverbs. The language associated with the recipient of most of the instructions in the discourse is "son" and "youth" (*naʿar*). Both of these are ambiguous in terms of chronological age. From the nature of the instruction, it seems as if these sons are married[10] and beginning a career. This would make the son at least an adolescent.

Even so, from the book's preface, I would argue that there are three groups addressed by the final form of the Book of Proverbs (identified by italic).

> Their purpose is to teach *people* wisdom and discipline,
>   to help them understand the insights of the wise.
> Their purpose is to teach people to live disciplined and
>   successful lives,
>   to help them do what is right, just, and fair.
> These proverbs will give insight to the *simple*,
>   knowledge and discernment to the young.
> Let the *wise* listen to these proverbs and become
>   even wiser.
>   Let those with understanding receive guidance
> by exploring the meaning in these proverbs and parables,
>   the words of the wise and their riddles.
> Fear of the LORD is the foundation of true knowledge,
>   but fools despise wisdom and discipline. (Prov. 1:2–7)

10. Although, according to V. Hamilton (*"naʿar," NIDOTTE* 3:124–27), *naʿar* indicates a nonmarried male of any age.

The preface tells us the purpose of the book as a whole and identifies three groups. The first part of the prologue (1:2–3) is addressed to "people" in general. This means that everyone is addressed by the book. However, the rest of the prologue may be divided into two parts, each of which specifies a different, narrower group of readers. The first are the simple-minded, also referred to as the young (1:4). The simple (*petî*) are neither wise nor foolish. They are, in a sense, unformed. They can do stupid things, to be sure, and sometimes they will be grouped with the fool (*kĕsîl*) or mocker (*lēṣ*) later in the book (e.g., 1:22). But the difference between the simple-minded and the fool and mocker may be summed up in one word: teachability. Fools "despise wisdom and discipline" (1:7), but the simpleminded in this context is "immature." The purpose of the Book of Proverbs toward this group made up of the immature is to develop them as people along the right path.

The second specific group mentioned in the prologue is the wise or, maybe better, the mature (1:5). They too may benefit from the book. It will "increase teaching" and in particular enhance their interpretive ability.

Thus, the Book of Proverbs, though seemingly narrowly addressed to the son, is for everyone, with one notable exception: the fool is excluded. Perhaps it would be more accurate to say that fools exclude themselves. After all, according to Prov. 1:7, wisdom begins with fear of the Lord, but a fool is defined, according to Ps. 14:1, by his or her rejection of God.

4. *Parents must discipline their children for their own good.* Here is where Proverbs gets dicey for a modern audience. Nevertheless, there can be no doubt that Proverbs teaches that discipline, sometimes physical, is appropriate in certain situations. Sometimes that last qualifier—"in certain situations"—is missed. After all, certain proverbs sometimes sound to a modern audience as if they insist on corporal punishment.

> Folly is bound up in the heart of a boy,
>   but the rod of discipline drives it far away. (22:15 NRSV)

> Do not withhold discipline from your children;
>   if you beat them with a rod, they will not die.

> If you beat them with a rod,
>> you will save their lives from Sheol. (23:13–14 NRSV)

> The rod and reproof give wisdom,
>> but a mother is disgraced by a neglected child. (29:15 NRSV)

This last proverb gives a different definition of "child neglect" than that found in modern Western society. According to this proverb, a neglected child is one who is not disciplined when it is necessary.

Reading these proverbs makes us realize that the Book of Proverbs allows for corporal punishment. Certainly, in light of the teaching of the rest of the book about gentleness, moderation, and so forth, we would expect that when corporal discipline is administered, it is done in moderation and for the betterment of the child, not as an act of retribution or for the parent to let off steam. In other words, these proverbs would not condone child abuse.

However, the other point I would make, based on the nature of the proverb, is that these proverbs *do not insist* on physical punishment. I remember how uncomfortable I was some twenty-five years ago when I was at the home of a young couple who insisted, on the basis of these proverbs, that they had to hit their young daughter with a ruler for a minor infraction. They were, after all, saving their child from Sheol. They even felt that it was wrong to spank rather than to use a rod.

A proverb depends on the situation and the child. One must take into account the child's nature, age, history, and much, much more. The important point is discipline, not the nature of the discipline.

Some of the passages that comment on the discipline of children come connected with a promise. One such text that has received fairly extensive discussion is 22:6:

> Direct your children onto the right path,
>> and when they are older, they will not leave it. (NLT)

> Train children in the right way,
>> and when they are old, they will not stray. (NRSV)

> Train a child in the way he should go,
>> and when he is old he will not turn from it. (NIV)

> Train a young person in his way,
> and when he gets older he will not turn aside from it.
> (literal translation)

There are a number of different possible understandings of this verse.[11] One common misunderstanding takes it as a directive to train a child according to the child's natural tendencies. Literally, "train a child in *his* way"—that is, the way of the child. Those who take this approach debate whether this is enlightened advice in pedagogy, which is extremely doubtful, or whether it is an observation delivered sarcastically—that is, if one trains a child in the way that the child wants, then that child will never depart from that way but will stick with his or her spoiled ways.

I think that the English versions get the correct sense even though they add words to make it clear: train children so that they get on the *right* (a word not in the Hebrew) path. This understanding certainly fits better with the broader teaching of the Book of Proverbs.

However, the connection between the imperative and the reward has been the source of pain to many parents, and it is on that subject that I focus my comments. Some parents labor over their children and try to raise them in a godly manner, but the children nonetheless go astray. Since all parents have inadequacies, self-doubt and self-incrimination set in. They ask themselves what they did as parents to lead to this painful conclusion.

However, we have already noted that in proverbs, rewards are not promises, at least in the short term. They are not guarantees. They are generally true principles. It is much more likely that one's children will grow up well if trained in a godly manner than if they are not.

5. *Parents must model godly behavior.* Discipline and instruction are not the only weapons in the parents' arsenal to wage war against the folly of the children in their charge. I choose the metaphor intentionally. The Book of Proverbs understands the

11. For a perceptive analysis of this verse in the midst of a number of different options, see T. Hildebrandt, "Proverbs 22:6a: Train Up a Child?" *GTJ* 9 (1988): 3–19.

young to be inherently foolish and that becoming wise takes
work:

> A youngster's heart is filled with foolishness,
>   but discipline will drive it away. (22:15)

A strong inducement to wise behavior for the young is what we
today would call "role modeling." Parents will live in such a
way that their children will mimic their behavior to their advantage:

> The godly walk with integrity;
>   blessed are the children who follow them. (20:7)

This is why, I believe, Proverbs recognizes the happy state of
the children of the godly:

> Evil people will surely be punished,
>   but the children of the godly will go free. (11:21)

In conclusion, with regard to the parent-child relationship in
Proverbs, I cite 17:6:

> Grandchildren are the crowning glory of the aged;
>   parents are the pride of their children.

When everything goes well in a family, all the generations take
joy and pride in their ancestors and descendants.

The Wife-Husband Relationship

The Book of Proverbs has extensive teaching not only on the
parent-child relationship but also on the marriage relationship. Most of the instruction comes from the first part of the
book, where the father is warning the son about the dangers
that threaten the marriage relationship. Thus, the teaching is
particularly concerned with young married couples. However,
as we will see, the advice that is given certainly is relevant to all
marriages.

Thus far, I have underlined the circumstantial truth of proverbial wisdom. The teaching on sexual relationships, however, comes with no escape clause. Adultery is always wrong. I will present Proverbs' teaching on loving the right woman by means of five instructions.

Avoid Immoral Women

As the father instructs his son in the first nine chapters, one dominant teaching emerges: avoid immoral women. Proverbs 2:16–22; 3:13–18; 4:4–9; 6:20–35; and the entirety of chapters 5 and 7 concern this theme. The father pulls out all the stops to bombard his son with this warning. After all, as he points out to his son, the consequences of this foolish act are dire.

> It will keep you from the immoral woman,
>> from the smooth tongue of the promiscuous woman.
> Do not lust for her beauty;
>> do not let her coy glances seduce you.
> For a prostitute will bring you to poverty,
>> but sleeping with another man's wife will cost you your life.
> Can a man scoop a flame into his lap
>> and his clothes not catch on fire?
> Can he walk on hot coals
>> and not blister his feet?
> So it is with the man who sleeps with another man's wife.
>> He who embraces her will not go unpunished. (6:24–29)

Who are these women whom the men are told to avoid? There are two: the prostitute and the promiscuous wife. These women, in Hebrew, are referred to as strange (*zārâ*; translated "immoral woman" in NLT) and foreign (*nokriyyâ*; translated "promiscuous woman" in NLT). They are strange and foreign because they act outside of the law and social convention, seeking sexual liaisons outside of marriage.

Sleeping with a prostitute or another person's wife is wrong, never right. However, there is a definite difference between the two, according to Proverbs. The difference is not one of relative rightness but of the practical consequences that flow from these actions. Sleeping with a prostitute will impoverish one, but sleeping with another man's wife may lead to one's death.

Considering the danger, why would anyone do it? The answer to this question explains why so much teaching is devoted to this subject: the temptation is great. The father does not try to minimize the temptation to the man; on the surface, it is an act that is hard to resist.

Interestingly, the most frequently cited reason for this temptation is the woman's speech. Her words to the man are flattering and seductive (2:16; 7:5). She wants the man and knows how to appeal to him. The immoral woman's mouth is attractive both for its sensuality and for uttering the words that men like to hear.

> The mouth of an immoral woman is a dangerous trap;
>   those who make the LORD angry will fall into it. (22:14)

But the attraction is also physical. The immoral woman in Prov. 7 is "seductively dressed" (7:10). He is also captivated by her pleasant smells and the possibility of embrace.

How can this great temptation be avoided? This leads to the second instruction.

Cultivate a Strong Relationship with Your Wife

> Drink water from your own cistern,
>   running water from your own well.
> Should your springs overflow in the streets,
>   your streams of water in the public squares?
> Let them be yours alone,
>   never to be shared with strangers.
> May your fountain be blessed,
>   and may you rejoice in the wife of your youth.
> A loving doe, a gracious deer—
>   may her breasts satisfy you always,
>   may you ever be captivated by her love.
> Why be captivated, my son, by an adulteress?
> Why embrace the bosom of another man's wife?
>   (Prov. 5:15–20 NIV)

The Book of Proverbs turns the young man's attention away from strange, foreign women, who seem so enticing, and toward his own wife. The imagery of the well for the woman and the streams of water for the man are erotic and suggest the ultimate in physical intimacy.

Appreciate the Joys of a Good Wife

The Book of Proverbs goes on to teach that a good wife is one of the most important things in life.

> The man who finds a wife finds a treasure;
>   he receives a gift from the LORD. (18:22)

Here I direct the reader to the well-known teaching on the virtuous woman in Prov. 31:1–31. Space does not allow me to exposit this rich passage, but it certainly explicates the benefits of a virtuous and capable wife.[12]

Be Aware of the Agony of a Bad Choice

But Proverbs is fully aware that not all wives are as supportive as the virtuous woman of Prov. 31. Indeed, there are women who are a hindrance rather than a help.

> But a disgraceful woman is like cancer in his bones. (12:4a)

Then, of course, there is a well-known series of "better than" proverbs that express the sadness of a bad match:

> A quarrelsome wife is as annoying
>   as constant dripping on a rainy day.
> Stopping her complaints is like trying to stop the wind
>   or trying to hold something with greased hands. (27:15–16; see
>   also 21:9, 19; 25:24)

Nowhere does Proverbs suggest that the young man abandon a bad wife. I believe that this teaching is, rather, a warning to young unmarried men not to place themselves in a bad relationship. They should be cautious and deliberate in their choice

---

12. For more, see the treatment in D. Allender and T. Longman III, *Intimate Allies* (Wheaton, Ill.: Tyndale House, 1995), 167–74.

of a life partner. In particular, they should be careful not to let a woman's physical beauty blind them to a bad personality.

> A beautiful woman who lacks discretion
>   is like a gold ring in a pig's snout. (11:22)

And in the context of the poem on the virtuous woman comes this:

> Charm is deceptive, and beauty does not last;
>   but a woman who fears the LORD will be greatly praised.
>   (31:30)

See the Human Reflections of Divine Realities

I will use this instruction to present the broader theological meaning of the Book of Proverbs, to which I referred at the outset. As the father instructs the son, he divides women into two contrasting groups. The father pits the wife against the promiscuous woman.

This divide reflects divine realities. As we read Prov. 1–9, the dominant metaphor is of life as a path. The addressee of the book, who in its original setting is a young man, is walking on the path and ultimately encounters two women. These women are called Wisdom and Folly. Wisdom is described at length in Prov. 8, but both women invite the reader to enter into an intimate relationship with them in Prov. 9, a chapter that serves as a pivot to the second part of the book.

> Wisdom has built her house;
>   she has carved its seven columns.
> She has prepared a great banquet,
>   mixed the wines,
>   and set the table.
> She has sent her servants to invite everyone to come.
>   She calls out from the heights overlooking the city.
> "Come in with me," she urges the simple.
>   To those who lack good judgment, she says,
> "Come, eat my food and drink the wine I have mixed.
> Leave your simple ways behind, and begin to live;
>   learn to use good judgment." (9:1–6)

The woman named Folly is brash.
   She is ignorant and does not know it.
She sits in her doorway
   on the heights overlooking the city.
She calls out to men going by
   who are minding their own business.
"Come in with me," she urges the simple.
   To those who lack good judgment, she says,
"Stolen water is refreshing;
   food eaten in secret tastes the best!"
But little do they know that the dead are there.
   Her guests are in the depths of the grave. (9:13–18)

Close study demonstrates that wives reflect the characteristics of the woman Wisdom and that promiscuous women reflect their leader, the woman Folly. But who are these two women?

Most scholars are willing to say that Wisdom is a personification of Yahweh's wisdom, but I would go further. Taking my cue from the location of their houses on the "heights overlooking the city," I suggest that ultimately they represent deity. Only the temple could be found on the heights of the city in an ancient Near Eastern town. Thus, the woman Wisdom represents Yahweh, and the woman Folly represents all the false deities of the surrounding nations. The young man must choose, ultimately, between these two. In this way, we can see how the Book of Proverbs is more than simply practical advice. The book is profoundly theological, connecting wisdom to relationship with Yahweh. After all, "fear of the Lord is the foundation of true knowledge."

The Book of Proverbs' perspective is practical, and we have seen all kinds of good advice about how to build a strong, cohesive family. But we should never forget that at the heart of the advice is wisdom, and wisdom is fundamentally a theological concept.

Wisdom involves relationship with God himself. Thus, we conclude this section by reading Prov. 24:3 with a rich theological understanding of wisdom:

A house is built by wisdom
   and becomes strong through good sense.

Through knowledge its rooms are filled
with all sorts of precious riches and valuables.[13]

Ecclesiastes and Job on the Family

The argument can be made that Proverbs lays the foundation for our understanding of wisdom, and then Ecclesiastes and Job keep us from overreading it. I often refer to these latter two books as canonical correctives to mechanical readings of the Book of Proverbs.

While it is true, as van Leeuwen has pointed out,[14] that a small number of proverbs do register the understanding that retributive justice does not always work out, it is possible to read the Book of Proverbs and come out with an overly optimistic view of the reward that comes to the godly and the curse that comes to the wicked. Job and Ecclesiastes keep us from treating the motive clauses of Proverbs as promises.[15]

The three friends of Job can be seen as people who treat the rewards of proverbs as promises rather than as generally true principles. Accordingly, they think not only that the wicked suffer but also that anyone who suffers must be wicked. As the Book of Job ridicules their viewpoint, so it ridicules any others who would promote a health-and-wealth gospel built on Proverbs.

Ecclesiastes is a more complicated book, and as such, its interpretation is more controversial; I cannot go into detail in the space allotted here.[16] In my estimation, Ecclesiastes is a book with two voices.[17] The more dominant voice is that of Qohelet, the Teacher, who concludes that life is without ultimate mean-

13. With the richer theological understanding of wisdom, we can see how this proverb expresses a thought similar to Psalm 127, a wisdom poem in its own right.

14. R. Van Leeuwen, "Wealth and Poverty: System and Contradiction in Proverbs," *HS* 33 (1992): 25–36.

15. B. Waltke, "Does Proverbs Promise Too Much?" *AUSS* 34 (1996): 319–26.

16. I share this view with others. See my *Ecclesiastes*, NICOT (Grand Rapids: Eerdmans, 1997).

17. See, most notably, the work of Michael V. Fox, in particular "Frame-Narrative and Composition in the Book of Qohelet," *HUCA* 48 (1977): 83–106; *Qohelet and His Contradictions*, JSOTSup 71 (Sheffield: Almond, 1989); *A Time to Tear Down and a Time to Build Up: A Rereading of Ecclesiastes* (Grand Rapids: Eerdmans, 1999).

ing in view of death and the inability to discern the time. He indeed looks for meaning in various areas, including wisdom, work, wealth, pleasure, and success, but each area comes up short. Death is the end of the story, and the best one can hope for are momentary respites from the harsh realities of life. This is the teaching of the so-called *carpe diem* passages in Ecclesiastes.

In light of the topic of this essay, it is interesting to see what Qohelet has to say about family relationships. A survey of Qohelet's comments about family relationships shows that he was ambivalent at best.

In the first place, Qohelet clearly saw advantages to companionship. While probably not written about marriage or the family directly, Eccles. 4:9–12 may be extended to include what is clearly the most intimate of all human relationships, the family:

> Two are better than one, for they can get a good return for their toil. For if one of them falls down, the other can help his friend up. But pity the person who falls when there is not another to help. Also, if two people lie down together, they keep warm; but how can one person keep warm? And though someone can overpower one person, two can resist the attacker. "A three-stranded cord does not quickly snap."

So at least theoretically, Qohelet would see relationship and certainly family as a solace in the midst of a hard and meaningless existence. However, other passages make one wonder whether he thought that this was actually possible. One passage that may indicate this is the much-discussed 7:25–29:

> I began to devote myself to understand and to explore and to seek wisdom and the sum of things, and to understand the evil of foolishness and the folly of madness. And I was finding: More bitter than death is the woman who is a snare, whose heart is a trap and whose hands are chains. The one who pleases God will escape her, but the one who is offensive will be captured by her.
>
> "Observe," Qohelet said, "this I have found: adding one thing to another to find the sum of things, which I am still seeking but not finding. I found one man out of a thousand, but I did not find a woman among all these. Only observe this: I have found that God made people upright, but they have sought out many devices.

So the most frequently heard voice in Ecclesiastes is ambiva-lent at best about relationship.

However, it is the second voice that is the canonical voice of the Book of Ecclesiastes. The words of a second, unnamed wise man frame the speech of Qohelet. He both introduces (1:1–11) and evaluates Qohelet (12:8–14). Again, space con-spires against a full discussion, but what is of interest to our topic is that this second, unnamed wise man is instructing his son (12:12) by use of Qohelet's speech. In a nutshell, he af-firms to his son that Qohelet speaks the truth as he describes the horrors of the world under the sun, but he also points his son beyond Qohelet's teaching, in the last two verses, when he states,

> The end of the matter. All has been heard. Fear God and keep his commandments, for this is the whole duty of humanity. For God will bring every deed into judgment, including every hidden thing, whether good or evil. (12:13–14)

The Song of Songs on the Family

Brevard Childs,[18] Francis Landy,[19] and others have called the Song of Songs a work of Wisdom literature—this in addition to, not in place of, its identification as love poetry. Others have re-jected this identification. Certainly, there is a clear difference between the Song of Songs and a conspicuously didactic work such as the Book of Proverbs. However, if wisdom is broadly conceived, as suggested by Childs and Landy, then a case can be made for the appropriateness of wisdom as descriptive of the Song of Songs. Wisdom is the application of God's will to the nitty-gritty of life. This, at least, is a partial perspective on the topic. By describing a love that is intense, exclusive, and faithful in spite of obstacles, the Song of Songs indirectly but passionately reveals God's will for that special relationship be-tween a man and a woman. Roland Murphy insightfully points

18. B. S. Childs, *Introduction to the Old Testament as Scripture* (Philadel-phia: Fortress, 1979), 573–75.

19. F. Landy, *Paradoxes of Paradise: Identity and Difference in the Song of Songs* (Sheffield: Almond, 1983), 33.

out that the Song of Songs might be read as an "explication of Prov. 30:19: 'the way of a man with a maiden.'"[20] It is certainly not out of keeping with Wisdom literature to note that explicit theological language is lacking in the Song of Songs, although, when read canonically, the book is rich in insight into the relationship between God and his people.[21] Jill Munro may be on the right track when she notices a wisdom connection in the relationship between the young woman and the chorus of other young women, whom she is instructing in the ways of love.[22]

In any case, the presence of the Song of Songs in the canon dispatches the idea that biblical love is all about spiritual communion and biblical marriage is all about commitment. No, the Song of Songs is an anthology of love poems that make it clear that romance and physical intimacy are part of God's will for the marriage relationship, and this is illustrated simply by citing one of the most intense of all the love poems in the collection:

> Set me like a seal on your heart,
>   like a seal on your arm.
> For stronger than death is love,
>   tenacious like the grave is jealousy.
> Its flame is an intense fire,
>   a god-like flame.
> Many waters are not able to extinguish love,
>   nor rivers flood it.
> Even if a person gave all the wealth of his house for love,
>   he would be completely despised. (8:6–7)[23]

In conclusion, this survey of Old Testament wisdom indicates much material that is relevant to our understanding of the family. The ideal is strong, cohesive families in which parents, children, husbands, and wives support each other in the midst of a chaotic world.

20. R. E. Murphy, *Wisdom Literature: Job, Proverbs, Ruth, Canticles, Ecclesiastes and Esther,* FOTL 13 (Grand Rapids: Eerdmans, 1981), 104.

21. This is argued in the lengthy introduction to T. Longman III, *Song of Songs,* NICOT (Grand Rapids: Eerdmans, 2001).

22. J. M. Munro, *Spikenard and Saffron: The Imagery of the Song of Songs,* JSOTSup 203 (Sheffield: Sheffield Academic Press, 1995), 146–47.

23. Longman, *Song of Songs,* 207.

5

Family in the Prophetic Literature

M. Daniel Carroll R.

Introduction: Challenges and Hermeneutical Considerations

The topic of this essay is a difficult one. The Prophetic literature of the Old Testament does not offer readers series of family-related laws as does the Pentateuch, developed scenes of family life similar to what is found in Genesis and Samuel–Kings, or the rich variety of materials of the Wisdom literature, such as the many exhortations and aphorisms of Proverbs, the soliloquies of Job, and the love songs of the Song of Songs. The first challenge for any study of the family in the Prophets, therefore, is to know where to look for relevant passages.

Within the broader world of biblical studies, another and very serious challenge comes from the fact that images of the family and lessons for family life that might be drawn from the Old Testament prophets sometimes are viewed in a negative manner. The Prophetic literature is condemned as reflecting—and, more insidiously, sanctifying even to our day—an unfair and destructive hierarchical and patriarchal view of the male-female relationship, the respective worth of each gender, and their potential roles within society.[1] Many feminist scholars have stridently condemned the picture of women and marriage that they have reconstructed from their analysis of several prophetic texts. This critique has been directed especially at two books: Hosea and Ezekiel.[2]

The account of the prophet's marriage to Gomer in Hos. 1–3 and the theological reflections generated there for Yahweh's relationship to Israel are said not to describe tender conjugal love—whether human or divine (a tack usually taken and expounded by evangelicals, for instance)—but rather the stereotypical response of an offended male of that ancient patriarchal culture whose prestige had been threatened by an incorrigible, wanton wife. The woman Israel is threatened physically, it is said, and publicly shamed (Hos. 2:2–13 [2:4–15 MT]) before being wooed back by Yahweh into a restored relationship (2:14–23 [2:16–25 MT]). The feminist indictment of Ezekiel is harsher. Chapters 16 and 23 repeat use of the harlot metaphor, but the punishment administered by the dishonored father-

1. See C. A. Newsom and S. H. Ringe, eds., *The Women's Bible Commentary*, rev. ed. (Louisville: Westminster John Knox, 1998); Alice Ogden Bellis, *Helpmates, Harlots, Heroes: Women's Stories in the Hebrew Bible* (Louisville: Westminster John Knox, 1994), 177–90; Carol J. Dempsey, *The Prophets: A Liberation-Critical Reading* (Minneapolis: Fortress, 2000); idem, *Hope amid the Ruins: The Ethics of Israel's Prophets* (St. Louis: Chalice, 2000), esp. 89–106.

2. See Renita J. Weems, *Battered Love: Marriage, Sex, and Violence in the Hebrew Prophets*, OBT (Minneapolis: Fortress, 1995); J. Cheryl Exum, "The Ethics of Biblical Violence against Women," in *The Bible in Ethics: The Second Sheffield Colloquium*, ed. J. W. Rogerson, M. Davies, and M. D. Carroll R., JSOTSup 207 (Sheffield: Sheffield Academic Press, 1995), 248–71; Athalaya Brenner, "Pornoprophetics Revisited: Some Additional Reflections," *JSOT* 70 (1996): 63–86. For the individual prophetic books, see Newsom and Ringe, eds., *The Women's Bible Commentary*. For Ezekiel, see Julie Galambush, *Jerusalem in the Book of Ezekiel: The City as Yahweh's Wife* (Atlanta: Scholars Press, 1992); Katheryn Pfisterer Darr, "Ezekiel's Justifications of God: Teaching Troubling Texts," *JSOT* 55 (1992): 97–117. For Hosea, see T. Drorah Setel, "Prophets and Pornography: Female Sexual Imagery in Hosea," in *Feminist Interpretation of the Bible*, ed. L. M. Russell (London: Basil Blackwell, 1985), 86–95; Yvonne Sherwood, *The Prostitute and the Prophet: Hosea's Marriage in Literary-Theoretical Perspective*, JSOTSup 212, Gender and Culture 2 (Sheffield: Sheffield Academic Press, 1996).

husband Yahweh appears to be more abusive (Ezek. 16:38–42; 23:24–35, 40–49). In addition, the descriptions of the sexual activity (metaphors for idolatry and foreign alliances) and the subsequent divine chastisement are said to verge on the voyeuristic and pornographic (16:15–18, 25–37; 23:1–22). As in the case of Hosea, male vengeance on the disrespectful women (who represent Jerusalem in Ezek. 16 and Israel and Judah in Ezek. 23) is meted out before restoration (16:59–63). For some feminists—not all—the cultural and ideological gap is simply too great to be bridged; for these scholars, the Old Testament's inherent weaknesses make it irredeemable or, at best, a deeply flawed and contradictory source. They argue that the biblical text, as well as the history of its interpretation, is androcentric, even misogynist.

Recent studies of the social life of ancient Israel have demonstrated that some of the modern feminist accusations against the Old Testament might be a bit misinformed and exaggerated. Archaeological data and comparative anthropological studies have led Carol Meyers and others to point out that women indeed did hold a position of some prestige within the Israelite household. What is more, women often performed a wide range of indispensable and highly skilled activities, which in fact demanded more technological expertise than did the typical tasks of males.[3] On the basis of a careful reading of the relevant Old Testament texts, Christopher Wright argues against the common misconception that wives were mere property of their husbands, chattel without rights or honor.[4] Happily, recent evangelical commentators on Hosea and Ezekiel have acknowl-

3. Carol Meyers, *Discovering Eve: Ancient Israelite Women in Context* (Oxford: Oxford University Press, 1988); idem, "The Family in Ancient Israel," in *Families in Ancient Israel*, ed. L. G. Perdue et al., The Family, Religion, and Culture (Louisville: Westminster John Knox, 1997), 1–47; Grace I. Emmerson, "Women in Ancient Israel," in *The World of Ancient Israel: Sociological, Anthropological and Political Perspectives*, ed. R. E. Clements (Cambridge: Cambridge University Press, 1989), 371–94; Victor H. Matthews and Don C. Benjamin, *Social World of Ancient Israel, 1250–587 B.C.E.* (Peabody, Mass.: Hendrickson, 1993), 22–36; Lawrence E. Stager and Philip J. King, *Life in Biblical Israel*, Library of Ancient Israel (Louisville: Westminster John Knox, 2001), 49–57.

4. Christopher J. H. Wright, *God's People in God's Land: Family, Land, and Property in the Old Testament* (Grand Rapids: Eerdmans; Exeter: Paternoster, 1990), 183–231.

edged the feminist critiques of these prophetic texts and have attempted to respond in sensitive ways from within a higher view of the authority and trustworthiness of the Bible.[5] Important evangelical works on hermeneutics also have sympathetically engaged in informed and creative ways with feminist interpretive practices, while at the same time developing the case for more responsible readings of the biblical text.[6]

It is beyond the scope of this essay to engage feminist scholarship in any depth in my attempt to glean material from the Prophetic literature for this study of the family. At the same time, however, these sorts of concerns should alert us to be more careful in our reading of these texts. Of course, reservations about the value of the Old Testament cannot be limited to feminists. The recent volume on Old Testament ethics by Cyril Rodd, *Glimpses of a Strange Land*, for instance, is dedicated primarily to highlighting how different the worldview and morality of the Old Testament are from ours.[7] For Rodd, the Old Testament reflects a time and a place (hence the title's allusion to a "strange land") so foreign and so limited by its context that it should not be allowed to have authority over modern readers.[8] These misgivings can serve to alert us to be wary of making too facile a jump to the needs of our con-

5. David Allen Hubbard, *Hosea*, TOTC 22A (Downers Grove, Ill.: InterVarsity, 1989), 43–45; Raymond C. Ortlund Jr., *Whoredom: God's Unfaithful Wife in Biblical Theology*, NSBT 2 (Grand Rapids: Eerdmans, 1996), 177–85; Duane A. Garrett, *Hosea, Joel*, NAC 19A (Nashville: Broadman & Holman, 1997), 124–33; Daniel I. Block, *Ezekiel 1–24*, NICOT (Grand Rapids: Eerdmans, 1997), 467–70. See also R. W. L. Moberly's thoughtful interaction with feminist readings of Gen. 22, which easily could be applied to the Prophetic literature, in his *The Bible, Theology, and Faith: A Study of Abraham and Jesus*, Cambridge Studies in Christian Doctrine 5 (Cambridge: Cambridge University Press, 2000), 162–83.

6. Anthony C. Thistleton, *New Horizons in Hermeneutics: The Theory and Practice of Transforming Biblical Reading* (Grand Rapids: Zondervan, 1992), 430–62; Kevin J. Vanhoozer, *Is There a Meaning in This Text? The Bible, the Reader, and the Morality of Literary Knowledge* (Grand Rapids: Zondervan, 1998), 167–68, 180–82, passim. Francis Watson uses the law-gospel distinction to develop the notion of an internal self-critique inherent within the Bible itself in his *Text, Church, and World: Biblical Interpretation in Theological Perspective* (Grand Rapids: Eerdmans, 1994), 155–240.

7. Cyril S. Rodd, *Glimpses of a Strange Land: Studies in Old Testament Ethics*, Old Testament Studies (Edinburgh: Clark, 2001).

8. Ibid., 271–329. For Rodd, issues dealing with women are just part of the larger problem (see pp. 250–70).

temporary context. The world (or, better, worlds) of ancient Israel truly is unlike ours, and the differences need to be recognized in any effort to appropriate the prophets for today.

How, then, are we to proceed? To begin with, in interpretation an important axiom is to recognize the differences between the world of the text and our own. Older texts on hermeneutics high-lighted the need to investigate historical backgrounds in order to better understand textual particulars. More recent hermeneutical theory, however, has demonstrated that the gap is more than just informational. To use the jargon of these more philosophical and literary approaches, a proper sense of the distance between the horizon of the text and the horizon of its modern readers and their communities is the prerequisite for an appropriate fusion of those two horizons.[9]

My first task in the first major section of this essay, therefore, is to point out some of the differences between family life in ancient Israel as reflected in the Prophetic Books and family life today. On the basis of this exercise in "contextual discernment," I will try to suggest some positive lessons for followers of Yahweh in the mod-ern world. The second major section will consider several of the family metaphors for God and his people in the Prophetic litera-ture that arose in the biblical world. That discussion will also deal briefly with the nature and limitations of metaphorical language in describing God. In sum, this essay will try to deal in an intro-ductory fashion with both the *methodological issues* related to using the prophets and some of the *constructive lessons* that this material can provide for the contemporary family.

Glimpses of Family Life . . . and Its Denunciation in the Prophets

A helpful starting point from which to begin to explore the world of the family within the Old Testament is the terminology

9. Hans-Georg Gadamer, *Truth and Method* (New York: Continuum, 1975), 263–67; Anthony C. Thistleton, *The Two Horizons: New Testament Hermeneu-tics and Philosophical Description* (Grand Rapids: Eerdmans, 1980), 51–84, 304–26, passim; idem, *New Horizons in Hermeneutics*, 556–620; Luis Alonso Schökel, *A Manual of Hermeneutics*, Biblical Seminar 54 (Sheffield: Sheffield Academic Press, 2001), 78–93.

or labels for various social and kinship institutions. A perusal of the Old Testament demonstrates that Israel divided its kinship structures into basically three levels (see, e.g., Josh. 7:16–18; Judg. 18:19).[10] The largest was the tribe (Hebrew *šēbeṭ* or *maṭṭeh*). The next subunit, the *mišpāḥâ* (which has been variously translated in the versions as "clan" or "family," and within more technical literature as a "protective association of families," "phratry," or "residential kinship group"), conveys the identity of a set of families linked by kinship ties to a common ancestor and living within a shared territorial boundary. In many cases, the "clan" was coterminous with a village or cluster of villages.

The third term is more pertinent to our concerns. The *bêt-ʾāb* (lit., "father's house") refers to the extended family. The nomenclature communicates its patrilineal (descent being reckoned through the male line) and patrilocal character. It included the descendants of the single living male head with his wife (or wives), his sons and their families, and grandsons and their families, as well as any unmarried or widowed daughters and other dependents (such as slaves or resident aliens). Marriages were arranged by these families and usually were endogamous to the *mišpāḥâ* (i.e., within the "clan"). It was also here within their families that everyone was trained in the traditions, rituals, and ethical mores of Israel's faith. In other words, the extended family provided the individual with the most basic sense of ethnic and religious identity, affections, and mutual responsibilities.

The Israel of the Old Testament was primarily a rural, agrarian society, even into the era of the divided monarchy that saw the rise and development of urban centers. These urban centers, as we will see shortly, are many times the target of the prophets' diatribes. In ancient Israel the extended family often lived in a series of connected or closely situated houses in what

10. Norman K. Gottwald, *The Tribes of Yahweh: A Sociology of the Religion of Liberated Israel, 1350–1050 B.C.E.* (Maryknoll, N.Y.: Orbis, 1979), 237–341; Wright, *God's People in God's Land*, 48–55; idem, "Family," *ABD* 2:762–63; Stager and King, *Life in Biblical Israel*, 36–40. Gottwald situates his discussion within a larger argument concerning the establishment of Israel as an egalitarian society in conscious contradistinction to the structures and values of the Canaanite city-state.

we might call a "multifamily compound" within the same village.[11] The standard Israelite home was what has been called a "pillared" (or "four room") house.[12] Apparently, these were of variable size—although small by modern standards—depending on a family's means, and of two stories. The first floor served primarily for processing food, cooking, and as a domestic stable; the second floor probably was where the family dined and slept. The economic basis of the extended family and the village usually was mixed farming and some livestock (usually sheep and goats) on the family's ancestral land (the *nahălâ*). Climactic variations, disease, high infant mortality rates, wars, and the difficult terrain made life a sustained struggle to survive. Gender and age-group roles in large measure were determined by the interdependent responsibilities that each member of the household had to contribute individually and corporately to help ensure that survival.

This kind of extended family structure, with all of its interconnected commitments and values, clearly differs from the nuclear family (whether of the two biological parents, single parents, blended families, and the like) and the concept of isolated individual rights that define so much of North American society. The routines of daily life of ancient Israel also were radically dissimilar in all sorts of ways from what most of us in modern North America are familiar with. Can that family world reflected in the biblical text, which seems so foreign to our experience today, inform the life of Christians and the church? I would say, "Yes, it can. Indeed, it must, as our holy Scripture." Even though that world is very different from ours, there are some significant enduring lessons to be drawn from that ancient and far-off context. One way of appreciating this task is to

11. Lawrence E. Stager, "The Archaeology of the Family in Ancient Israel," *BASOR* 260 (1985): 1–35; Carol Meyers, *Discovering Eve;* idem, "Family in Ancient Israel"; Leo G. Perdue, "The Israelite and Early Jewish Family: Summary and Conclusions," in Perdue et al., eds., *Families in Ancient Israel,* 163–222; cf. Matthews and Benjamin, *Social World of Ancient Israel,* 1–154.

12. Stager, "Archaeology of the Family"; John S. Holladay Jr., "House, Israelite," *ABD* 3:308–18; Edward F. Campbell, "Archaeological Reflections on Amos's Targets," in *Scripture and Other Artifacts: Essays on the Bible and Archaeology in Honor of Philip J. King,* ed. M. D. Coogan, J. C. Exum, and L. E. Stager (Louisville: Westminster John Knox, 1994), 32–52; Stager and King, *Life in Biblical Israel,* 28–35.

look at some of the kinds of family arenas that are briefly described but severely criticized in the Prophetic literature. In what follows, I will point to two such groups of scenes that can serve as guides for reflection on families today.

Worship

The prophets, as is the Old Testament as a whole, are very exercised by what they deem the unacceptable religious life of the people of God. It is not surprising, therefore, to find that a number of passages that do present glimpses of the Israelite family tend to concentrate on their religious practices.

In the last several years the academic literature based on archaeological findings dealing with the religion of ancient Israel has been increasing at an almost exponential rate.[13] Scholars offer different taxonomies in their categorizing of religious beliefs and practices within Israel and have developed theories about the rise of monotheism; there are also ongoing debates over the interpretation of the data. It is not necessary for us to review and assess those issues here. For our purposes it is enough to point out that the evidence, whether material or epigraphic (including the biblical texts), reveals the coexistence of a state cult, with its official rituals and personnel at the central shrine in the capital city, and more local worship areas, such as smaller formal sanctuaries, village and domestic shrines, and pilgrimage sites. Excavations across Palestine, and even in Jerusalem itself, have produced a wide assortment of cult objects, such as pillars (the *maṣṣēbôt*), altars, and various kinds of figurines (such as those of a horse and rider, the bull, and a goddess holding her breasts). It is plain that the religion of the Israelite family could be very complex, with belief in Yahweh

13. Significant sources include John S. Holladay, "Religion in Israel and Judah under the Monarchy," in *Ancient Israelite Religion: Essays in Honor of Frank Moore Cross*, ed. P. D. Miller Jr., P. D. Hanson, and S. D. McBride (Philadelphia: Fortress, 1987), 249–99; Othmar Keel and Christoph Uehlinger, *Gods, Goddesses, and Images of God in Ancient Israel*, trans. T. H. Trapp (Minneapolis: Fortress, 1998); Patrick D. Miller, *The Religion of Ancient Israel*, Library of Ancient Israel (Louisville: Westminster John Knox, 2000); Stager and King, *Life in Biblical Israel*, 319–81; Mark S. Smith, *The Early History of God: Yahweh and the Other Deities in Ancient Israel*, 2d ed. (San Francisco: Harper & Row, 2002).

being held along with the veneration of family gods, fertility deities, and perhaps even ancestors. The theological constructs and religious practices would demonstrate differing degrees of heterodoxy, depending on a host of particular national sociopolitical circumstances, foreign influences, and local histories and customs. Several prophetic passages can serve to highlight this troubling amalgam of beliefs in the families of ancient Israel.

The prophet Hosea, for instance, presents a frontal attack on the religious abominations of the northern kingdom in the eighth century. Scholars debate whether he is hitting at a syncretistic Yahwism or a separate Baal cult. There is also disagreement over whether the Baal cult included "sacred prostitution" within its ritual as part of an effort of sympathetic magic to facilitate fertility.[14] Again, it is not our goal to define with precision the nature of the worship that is condemned. What is of interest to us is the people whom the prophet mentions in Hos. 4:13–14. Here Hosea indicts the men of Israel,[15] who, along with their daughters and daughters-in-law, are involved in idolatrous worship on the high places that apparently included sexual promiscuity. Here family religion has gone awry, as the male heads of the households, in complicity with the women, participate in perverse activity related to non-Yahwistic religious practices. Another enigmatic passage is Amos 2:7–8, where father and son "go into the [same] girl" and drink wine gained unjustly, all within the context of some sort of religious practice.[16] Once more we cannot be totally certain of the nature of the activity that is condemned or whether this is a reference to a distorted worship of Yahweh or to a syncretistic cult, but the faith of the family again produces unacceptable re-

14. Scholars are increasingly questioning this interpretation. See Karel van der Toorn, "Female Prostitution in Payment of Vows in Ancient Israel," *JBL* 108, no. 2 (1989): 193–205; idem, "Prostitution," *ABD* 5:505–13; Phyllis A. Bird, "'To Play the Harlot': An Inquiry into an Old Testament Metaphor," in her *Missing Persons and Mistaken Identities: Women and Gender in Ancient Israel* (Minneapolis: Fortress, 1997), 219–36.

15. This could be a reference to the men of Israel in general or perhaps more specifically the priests, who earlier in Hos. 4 had been the focus of his critique.

16. Note the mention of profaning Yahweh's name in v. 7 and of the altar and "house of their god" in v. 8.

ligious and moral behavior. Mention can be made here, too, of Mal. 2:13–14, which says that some older men are leaving the wives of their youth, those women with whom they had a marriage covenant, in order to marry others, perhaps the pagan women spoken of in the preceding lines ("the daughter of a foreign god" [2:11–12]).[17]

Jeremiah 7:16–19 describes the involvement of the entire family in the worship of the Queen of Heaven. This same practice continued after the fall of Jerusalem in 586 B.C.E. to the Babylonians. The prophet reproves the continuation of this idolatry by those who had escaped to Egypt after the assassination of Gedaliah, the governor appointed by the empire (Jer. 44:15–25). These two passages obviously raise questions concerning the specific identity of the Queen of Heaven[18] and the place of women in the religious life of Israel in general.[19] The relevant point for us, however, is that all of the family members are involved in what the prophet considers an abomination and that the children are being socialized into this worldview and worship. Along with the prophet Zephaniah (1:5), Jeremiah also criticizes (19:12–13; 32:29) the devotion to the "starry host" and other gods.[20] Both prophets say that the offerings to these deities occur on the roofs of the people's houses. Although specific family members are not mentioned in these passages, one might very well assume that various, if not all, family members shared in some manner in this activity.

17. It is possible that these two pericopes refer to two distinct sins, so that marrying foreign women and the divorces are unrelated. Since some scholars do connect the two, however, we mention this possibility at this juncture. For an extended treatment, see Gordon P. Hugenberger, *Marriage as a Covenant: Biblical Law and Ethics as Developed from Malachi*, VTSup 52 (Leiden: Brill, 1994; reprint, Grand Rapids: Baker, 1998).

18. In addition to the sources listed above in n. 13, see Susan Ackerman, "'And the Women Knead Dough': The Worship of the Queen of Heaven in Sixth-Century Israel," in *Gender and Difference in Ancient Israel*, ed. P. L. Day (Minneapolis: Fortress, 1989), 109–24; idem, *Under Every Green Tree: Popular Religion in Sixth-Century Judah*, HSM 46 (Atlanta: Scholars Press, 1992), 5–35.

19. See Phyllis A. Bird, "The Place of Women in the Israelite Cultus," and "Israelite Religion and the Faith of Israel's Daughters: Reflections on Gender and Religious Definition," in *Missing Persons and Mistaken Identities*, 81–102, and 103–20, respectively; Miller, *Religion of Ancient Israel*, 201–6.

20. See Keel and Uehlinger, *Gods, Goddesses, and Images of God*, 283–372.

Another heinous religious ritual practiced by some was child sacrifice. Isaiah (57:3–13), Jeremiah (7:30–32; 19:4–6; 32:35), and Ezekiel (16:21; 20:31; 23:39) denounce this cult.[21] The evidence seems to indicate that child sacrifice was more of a royal prerogative, but others also performed it in times of severe crisis (such as a famine or siege). Isaiah 57 might also allude to a cult of the dead, where the departed were fed (note vv. 6–7, 9)—a practice described more explicitly in other passages (Isa. 8:19–20; 65:2–5). Scholars disagree about the time at which veneration of the ancestors appeared in Israel.[22] For those of us who come from a Latin American background, these scenes are reminiscent of the traditions of Roman Catholic popular religion, in which everyone goes annually on *el día de los muertos* (November 1, All Souls' Day) to the family burial plot in the cemetery and shares a meal on the graves of deceased loved ones.

In ancient Israel, religion concentrated on dealing with the multiple insecurities of the context, whether those threats came from the natural environment, personal tragedies, or national sociopolitical realities. In a culture that was overwhelmingly rural and agrarian, it is not surprising that special concern focused on the birth of children (especially males), the fertility of the land and animals, the fear of the uncertainties concerning death and the dead, and protection from disease and external enemies in war. The various kinds of religious life at all levels—although our attention has been on the family—strayed from pure faith in Yahweh and the proper exercise of rituals prescribed in the law to absorb beliefs and customs from the religions of neighboring peoples. The family, which had been des-

21. See Ackerman, *Under Every Green Tree*, 101–63, 165–212; Smith, *Early History of God*, 171–81.

22. See Ackerman, *Under Every Green Tree*, 143–52; Theodore J. Lewis, *Cults of the Dead in Ancient Israel and Judah*, HSM 39 (Atlanta: Scholars Press, 1989); Elizabeth Bloch-Smith, *Judahite Burial Practices and Beliefs about the Dead*, JSOTSup 123 (Sheffield: Sheffield Academic Press, 1992); Stager and King, *Life in Biblical Israel*, 376–81; Smith, *Early History of God*, 162–71. For a more reserved perspective, see Brian B. Schmidt, *Israel's Beneficent Dead: Ancestor Cult and Necromancy in Ancient Israelite Religion and Tradition* (Winona Lake, Ind.: Eisenbrauns, 1994). Scholars debate the nature and role of mourning rituals associated with the *marzēaḥ* feast (Amos 6:4–6; Jer. 16:5–9), which probably would have been limited to male members of well-to-do households.

ignated a primary locus for catechesis and the celebration of the Sabbath and the feasts, in large measure failed in its responsibility to help train up Israel to be a distinct people under God.

Ethical Practices

The prophets perhaps are best known for their diatribes against the injustice and oppression in Israel and Judah. Interestingly, what is almost universally forgotten in discussions of prophetic ethics is that the Old Testament consistently relates its ethical ideals and demands to the extended family. Morality was closely bound up with kinship relationships.[23]

To begin with, there are a number of laws dedicated to helping preserve the ancestral land within the family and thus helping to ensure its well-being and continued existence. Here we could mention, for instance, the levirate law (Deut. 25:5–10), whereby a member of a widow's husband's family took her as a wife in order to provide a rightful male heir to the property. Another safeguard was the legislation concerning the kinsman redeemer (the *gō'ēl*), who was expected to buy back property or secure the release of one who had fallen into debt (Lev. 25:25–55). The eligibility of those responsible for these measures began with the debtor's brother and then moved out progressively to wider circles within the clan. We see the prophet Jeremiah performing this duty in his book (32:6–15).

Households that received those sold into debt slavery were to treat fellow Israelites humanely. In addition, the Sabbatical year of release for slaves and property (Exod. 21:1–11; Deut. 15:1–18) and the Jubilee were supposed to provide periodic opportunities for families that had come into difficult straits because of debt to have those debts forgiven and their ancestral property restored so that they might have the chance to try again to sustain themselves. The law detailed several other ways that families might respond to the poor among them,

23. See especially Wright, *God's People in God's Land;* Perdue, "Israelite and Early Jewish Family," 192–203; Raymond Westbrook, *Property and Family in Biblical Law*, JSOTSup 113 (Sheffield: Sheffield Academic Press, 1991); cf. Frank M. Cross, "Kinship and Covenant in Ancient Israel," in *From Epic to Canon: History and Literature in Ancient Israel* (Baltimore: Johns Hopkins University Press, 1998), 3–21.

which included widows, orphans, and resident aliens. For example, they were to leave gleanings in the fields after the harvest (Deut. 24:19–21), invite the destitute to participate with them in the celebration of the national festivals (Deut. 16:9–14), and contribute a triennial tithe for the poor (Deut. 14:28–29; 26:12).

So central is the concept of the extended family, both in the literal sense and in its metaphorical extension to characterize the entire nation as an extended family under Yahweh, that Waldemar Janzen has structured his recent book on Old Testament ethics around what he calls the "familial paradigm."[24] The three components of the paradigm he develops are life (its preservation and enhancement), the possession of land and the enjoyment of its *shalom*, and hospitality. This familial background to ethics might encourage a reconsideration of the prophetic critique of the injustice and oppression within Israel and Judah.

In many ways the rise of the monarchy brought profoundly negative changes to the social welfare of the people of God and greatly impacted family life. Scholars have proposed a number of explanations for the shape and tenor of these changes.[25] Some speak of the "Canaanization" of the monarchy, such that a set of very different political perspectives that contradicted the original equitable values of Israel was incorporated by the nascent kingdoms. Others ground their theories in social-science studies and argue that the development of the monarchy was accompanied by the evolution of a form of capitalism. Still others have done more comparative work and point to the patronage and land-grant systems of surrounding governments (such as Egypt or Assyria) as the models adopted by Israel and Judah.

24. Waldemar Janzen, *Old Testament Ethics: A Paradigmatic Approach* (Louisville: Westminster John Knox, 1994).

25. For surveys, see John Andrew Dearman, *Property Rights in the Eighth-Century Prophets*, SBLDS 106 (Atlanta: Scholars Press, 1988), 1–17; M. Daniel Carroll R., *Contexts for Amos: Prophetic Poetics in Latin American Perspective*, JSOTSup 132 (Sheffield: Sheffield Academic Press, 1992), 22–47; Lester L. Grabbe and Robert D. Haak, eds., *"Every City Shall Be Forsaken": Urbanism and Prophecy in Ancient Israel and the Near East*, JSOTSup 330 (Sheffield: Sheffield Academic Press, 2001). Cf. Meyers, *Discovering Eve*, 189–96.

Whatever the correct reconstruction of the sociopolitical and economic conditions, the coming of the monarchy forever altered the landscape. With the establishment of the state came the imposition of taxes and forced labor. New internal markets and international trade led to changes in the choice of crops and use of the arable land. Production of any number of goods and products became more specialized and centralized. In addition, the personnel needs and the maintenance requirements of the royal courts and the growing cadre of officials distributed throughout both kingdoms, as well as the changes in national economic organization and policies, made migration to the towns and larger urban centers more attractive. The fall of the northern kingdom in the last quarter of the eighth century also led to a large migration south into Judah and resulted in the swelling of the population of the cities, especially Jerusalem. In other words, political, economic, and demographic factors increasingly shaped the life of the Israelite household.

On the one hand, a significant portion of the population (we cannot be sure of the percentage) fell into poverty through loss of their ancestral lands and removal from the traditional care offered by the extended family. Whatever the primary reason or combination of causes for this dispossession—whether the death of the heads of families and their sons as war casualties, crop failures, drought, disease, economic injustice, royal confiscation of property, or market manipulations—it is clear that a poor "underclass" arose.[26] In multiple passages the prophets decry the abuse suffered by widows, orphans, and the poor (e.g., Isa. 1:17, 23; 10:1–2; Jer. 5:26–29; 22:3; Zech. 7:10; Mal. 3:5). They denounce how the destitute are being bought and sold in debt slavery (Amos 2:6; 8:6). Jeremiah describes the temporary release of those in slavery who continue to be pawns of the powerful even in the last days before the destruction of Jerusalem by the Babylonian armies (Jer. 34:8–22).

On the other hand, while some families suffered, others benefited from, and exploited, those in need. Isaiah mocks the wealthy women of Zion who now parade their fineries in the

---

26. I realize that this is a modern concept that can communicate a host of connotations. No technical meaning is meant, however; hence the quotation marks.

streets but who one day themselves will be impoverished, widowed, and humiliated (Isa. 3:16–4:1). Amos calls this same sort of women in the northern capital, Samaria, "cows of Bashan." These are the women who, while demanding drink from their husbands, crush the poor (Amos 4:1; cf. 6:4–6).[27] Families with means accumulate properties (although the text does not specify how) and take advantage of those who are unable to hold on to their homes and fields (Isa. 5:8; Mic. 2:1–2; cf. 1 Kings 21).

The moral indignation of the prophets is consistently connected to the unacceptable worship of Yahweh. With one accord they declare that there can be no true faith in the God of Israel without ethics (e.g., Isa. 1:10–2:5; Jer. 7:1–15; Amos 4:4–5; 5:4–6, 11–24; Hos. 6:4–6; Mic. 6:6–8; Mal. 2:10–3:15). As I have developed elsewhere,[28] what makes this religious world of ancient Israel so perverse and self-destructive is that the whole nation believed that this state of things was how it should be. It was not only the rich and powerful who crowded the sanctuaries and praised Yahweh; so did those who were the victims of the very socioeconomic system that they believed God had sanctified and would protect against foreign invasion. They too had invested in the lie, in the cruel illusions of a national god of blessing of their own creation. In other words, the lack of ethics was compounded by religious confusion and contradictions.

In a sense, then, we have come full circle. We have returned to the problem of religion with which I began the discussion in this section. In the inseparable spheres of the moral life and religious beliefs and practices, we have found that, at least on the basis of what we can see in the Prophetic literature, the state of the family in ancient Israel in many ways was not good. The

27. Note David J. A. Clines's ideological critique of the prophet's diatribe against the rich, which Clines feels might not be a fair characterization of the actual life of the wealthy. This hermeneutics of suspicion could be placed alongside some feminist approaches. See his "Metacommentating Amos," in *Of Prophets' Visions and the Wisdom of Sages: Essays in Honour of R. Norman Whybray on His Seventieth Birthday*, ed. H. A. McKay and D. J. A. Clines, JSOTSup 162 (Sheffield: Sheffield Academic Press, 1993), 142–60.

28. Carroll R., *Contexts for Amos*, 273–77; "'For So You Love to Do': Probing Popular Religion in the Book of Amos," in *Rethinking Contexts, Rereading Texts: Contributions from the Social Sciences to Biblical Interpretation*, ed. M. D. Carroll R., JSOTSup 299 (Sheffield: Sheffield Academic Press, 2000), 168–89.

wide range of responsibilities before Yahweh, fellow family members, and the nation was neglected and distorted. The pressures of the moment, influences of the surrounding cultures, and human greed all contributed to distort what Janzen calls the "familial paradigm." It is here, I believe, that there are lessons for us today, although we are very far removed from the world of the prophets.

Christian families and their churches need to honestly assess the nature of their faith and ethics. Hard questions need to be asked: Are we nurturing our young in worship acceptable to God, or are we more concerned with entertaining them and keeping them interested in doing church activities? Can we mentor our children even as we delegate so much of their training in the Scripture and Christian life to professionals and separate ourselves from them in our worship services in the proliferation of specialty services for children, youth, and young adults? How is the culture informing and shaping the worship? Are we creating a god of our own choosing, one who wonderfully combines the qualities of a cosmic therapist, marriage counselor, capitalist CEO, and staunch defender of the American way of life but who never makes demands on our morality, lifestyle, and ideology? As we "dumb down" our churches and concentrate our energies in worship on emotive celebration, might we not at the same time be raising up a view of God and the Christian life that would receive the same kind of harsh and bitter denunciation that those prophets of long ago directed at Israel and Judah? What is more, in a society such as this one in the United States, where families are fragmented in so many ways, where the media glorify the independence of children at the expense of incompetent parents, where marriage is reduced to convenience and social contracts, where families are pounded with the ideal of the interminable acquisition of material things, and where the elderly are sent away, might there not also be food for thought regarding the positive contributions of the extended family, which would hold in high regard mutual affection, care of the weak, and moral accountability?

We cannot return to the patrilineal and patrilocal customs of ancient Israel, but we can learn many constructive values from that extended family structure. The extended family is the ideal of some of the immigrant communities here. The majority culture could afford to watch and learn from them, but perhaps those who have come from Hispanic, African, and Asian backgrounds, too, are now buying into the lures of suburbia and so, eventually, will inherit its deep dysfunction.

Can we find important material on the family in the Prophetic Books? The answer is yes, but what we encounter ultimately is a searching and very uncomfortable mirror whose relevance endures and continues to resonate across time.

Family Metaphors in the Prophets

Thus far, the portraits that the Prophetic literature have offered us have been universally negative. As we now turn to the various metaphors based on the family, there will be positive models upon which to draw, but contrary images and lessons will surface as well.

In general terms, a metaphor is a comparison drawn between two entities and is grounded in analogy. The similarities, however, never can be total, so one needs to be aware of how each side of the analogy is distinctive and different from the other. Nor is a metaphor static, as its nuances and impact can change over time. Because of the finiteness of human experience and categories of understanding, humans can speak about Yahweh only through the use of metaphors. At the same time, no one metaphor can fully capture the essence and activity of the boundless character of God.[29] Hence, the Old Testament utilizes a wide variety of metaphors to describe Yahweh. They all must be held in combination and in tension to avoid reducing Yahweh's person to one aspect or unwisely exaggerating one over the others. Each metaphor is counterbalanced and complemented by the theological richness of this variety. Scholars working with metaphorical language in the Bible increasingly are beginning to consciously appeal to more sophisticated models of metaphor in order to establish better theo-

29. See the discussion in Walter Brueggemann, *Theology of the Old Testament: Testimony, Dispute, Advocacy* (Minneapolis: Fortress, 1997), 117–313, esp. 229–66.

retical foundations for their analysis of texts. This trend is evident, for example, among those investigating the marriage metaphor in the Prophets.[30]

The extended family was one of the most fruitful sources for metaphors in ancient Israel for communicating the nature of their relationship to Yahweh and the roles of each party in that relationship.[31] In that culture the bonds of the family were particularly strong, so it was appropriate and significant that the (covenant) relationship between the deity and his chosen people was expressed in these terms.[32] In what follows, because of space limitations, I am able to highlight only some of this material and pertinent passages.

To begin with, Yahweh could be envisioned as the *father* of Israel. In two passages the people of God appeal to his compassion as the father of the nation. They suffer because of his judgment, but even as they wonder how Yahweh has kept himself hidden from them, they can boldly turn to him and make a claim on his affection. He is their creator and a father greater than Abraham (Isa. 63:16; 64:8 [64:7 MT]).[33] Although Yahweh is not often called "father" explicitly in the Prophets, the parent-child relationship is made evident by the fact that Israel many

30. For a feminist perspective, see Galambush, *Jerusalem in the Book of Ezekiel*, 4–20; Weems, *Battered Love*, 1–11. For a nonfeminist perspective, see N. Stienstra, *YHWH Is the Husband of His People: Analysis of a Biblical Metaphor with Special Reference to Translation* (Kampden: Kok Pharos, 1993), 17–69; R. Abma, *Bonds of Love: Methodic Studies of Prophetic Texts with Marriage Imagery (Isaiah 50:1–3 and 54:1–10, Hosea 1–3, Jeremiah 2–3)*, Studia Semitica Neerlandica (Assen: Van Gorcum, 1999), 7–13.

31. A helpful survey of the various family metaphors can be found in Leo G. Perdue, "The Household, Old Testament Theology, and Contemporary Hermeneutics," in Perdue et al., eds., *Families in Ancient Israel*, 225–34.

32. The covenant background is argued forcefully by, e.g., Wright, *God's People in God's Land*; Stienstra, *YHWH Is the Husband of His People*; Abma, *Bonds of Love*; Cross, "Kinship and Covenant in Ancient Israel." The dating of the covenant idea has been an issue of scholarly debate for over a century. We would hold to an early date and see the various covenants as the theological foundations of the bond between Yahweh and Israel from the very beginning.

33. Another verse that might appeal to Yahweh as father is Mal. 2:10. Commentators debate whether the question "Have we not all one father?" refers to God or to Abraham. Interestingly, as in the two passages in Isaiah, one finds a cluster of images that includes Yahweh, Abraham, and creation.

times is referred to as his *son,* or the people as his *children,* or Jerusalem as his *daughter.*[34]

It is important to remember the cultural (and biblical) demand that children respect their father as a backdrop for Yahweh's insistence on obedience. Israel is to follow his statutes and to live a life worthy of the calling as the firstborn son in every dimension of their national existence. But Israel has been a stubborn and rebellious son, and Jerusalem a wayward daughter. According to the penalties established in the law, such a son must be punished (the most extreme form of which would be execution [Deut. 21:18–21]).[35] Yahweh must respond to this sort of behavior, yet it is disconcerting to him. He had raised Israel since birth and provided for every need, but now the people are worse than an animal—at least an ass knows its master (Isa. 1:3)! He expected the nation to respond to his fatherly love (Jer. 3:19), but while they call him "father," they ignore him and do evil (Jer. 3:5; Hos. 11:1–7). He had "found" Jerusalem as a newborn baby, when she had been abandoned and was covered with blood. Under his care she had grown up to be a beautiful daughter, but now as an adult she had left his ways and forgotten his exquisite care to chase after lovers (Ezek. 16:1–19).

Yahweh takes his role as father with the utmost seriousness and expresses his sense of betrayal and disappointment in passionate terms. Nevertheless, even as he judges his people, he laments the necessity of the discipline and the devastating afflic-

34. These designations lead into discussions concerning the gender of nations and cities in the ancient Near East, Israel, and Judah. Note the survey in Galambush, *Jerusalem in the Book of Ezekiel,* 20–59; Abma, *Bonds of Love,* 20–23. I agree with Abma that the phenomenon of the personification of (capital) cities as females in the ancient Near East and in Israel is grounded not only in the notion of a marriage between the city and its patron deity but also in the fact that the city at the same time could be viewed as the mother of the populace and as a daughter of the god.

35. This sort of law raises the question of whether the prescribed penalties were taken literally and as mandatory or whether they functioned more as guidelines for establishing limits that would be considered in deliberations and according to the discretion of the elders or judges. See Henry McKeating's important article, "Sanctions against Adultery in Ancient Israelite Society, with Some Reflections on the Methodology in the Study of Old Testament Ethics," *JSOT* 11 (1979): 57–72.

tion it will bring. Yahweh likens the misery that the people will suffer at the hand of the invading armies to the excruciating pain that his "Daughter of Zion" will endure in childbirth (Jer. 4:31; Mic. 4:10; cf. Jer. 14:17–18). The judgment, however, is not his final word. The depth of Yahweh's commitment to his son (and daughter) is demonstrated by the announcement that he will restore the violated relationship. Precisely because he is the father of Israel, he will bring them back home to the land and nurture them again (Jer. 31:9). "How can I give you up, Ephraim? How can I turn you over, Israel?" he says (Hos. 11:8). This renewal in that future day will bring shouts of joy. Jerusalem, the Daughter of Zion, will once again sing in gladness (Zeph. 3:14; Zech. 9:9), because she will once again see the salvation of her God and enjoy his presence in her midst (Isa. 52:1–2; 62:11).

There are a few passages that suggest that Yahweh also could be considered Israel's *mother*. The issue of Yahweh as mother, or at least as (a male deity) manifesting what are thought to be traditional maternal images,[36] is not only theological but also historical and archaeological. Scholars debate the possible geographical-cultural provenance of such a religious idea and sometimes link this notion within the discussion of the worship of the goddess/Asherah in the religion of Israel.[37] The key passages are Isa. 46:3–4; 49:13–15; and 66:12–14. Each of these passages highlights Yahweh's loving care and affectionate encouragement to a people who felt abandoned by him as a result of the judgment of the exile. Just as a mother cannot desert the child she carried in her womb, so Yahweh will not leave this nation he had "carried since your birth" in Egypt and had faithfully sustained since then. Unlike the metaphor of Yahweh as father and husband, the image of God as mother does not have any punitive elements attached to it.

36. A pioneer work is Phyllis Trible, *God and the Rhetoric of Sexuality* (Philadelphia: Fortress, 1978).

37. For discussions of the gender imagery and roles assigned to Yahweh against the background of the ancient Near East, see Smith, *Early History of God*, 137–47. For the goddess/Asherah, see the sources in n. 13 above and Judith M. Hadley, *The Cult of Asherah in Ancient Israel and Judah: Evidence for a Hebrew Goddess*, University of Cambridge Oriental Publications 57 (Cambridge: Cambridge University Press, 2000).

In addition to his role as a parent within the family relationship, Yahweh was also the *husband* of Israel. Hence the nation was his *wife*. The key passages for this metaphor are Jer. 2–4, Hos. 1–3, and Ezek. 16 and 23. As I mentioned in the introduction, these chapters have been the focal point of feminists' critique of the ideology of the Prophetic Books, and others have responded to their observations in detail. But I do want to make three comments in passing. First, it is methodologically suspect to ignore the purpose of prophetic rhetoric. It is not uncommon for the prophets to use vivid metaphors that have violent connotations (e.g., Yahweh as a ravaging lion).[38] The metaphors are designed to communicate the reality of the holy passion of God for the submission of his people to his will and to convey the horror of the war that awaited the nation. Extreme and intentionally exaggerated images (such as the public exposure of the woman) served to generate disgust for the sin that the prophets were condemning and arouse fear of the coming judgment.

To appreciate the nature and role of metaphor leads me to the second point. It is clear to the careful reader that the metaphors are more concerned about impact than exactness. For example, although in Hosea, Jeremiah, and Ezek. 16 Yahweh is clearly the monogamous and loyal husband of Israel, in Ezek. 23 he is said to have married two sisters, Jerusalem and Samaria. Also, he will betroth her to himself again after she repents. Does that mean Israel will once again be a virgin?

Third, and as a logical implication of these first two observations, one needs to be careful about simplistically taking these rhetorically driven metaphors as the source for a sociohistorical reconstruction of what married life actually was like in ancient Israel (i.e., to use these images as a basis for saying that men systematically mistreated their wives) or for positing theological statements about the character of Yahweh (to claim that they are proof that he is an abusive deity caught within the web of a patriarchal culture).

As in the case of the father metaphor, the metaphor of Yahweh as husband expresses his profound love for Israel as well

---

38. See Pedro Jaramillo Rivas, *La injusticia y la opresión en el lenguaje figurado de los profetas* (Navarra, Spain: Verbo Divino, 1992).

as his dismay at her pursuing other gods with which to have a relationship. This unfaithfulness leads Yahweh to humble Israel, to abandon her for a time, and send her away. But like the father who goes beyond the cultural expectations to get his son (or daughter) back, Yahweh as Israel's husband will woo her again. He will take back the wife, who had left and deserted the home. Here Yahweh goes beyond what was stipulated in the law: he remarries the divorced woman (Deut. 24:1–4; Isa. 50:1–3; 54:1–10; Jer. 3:1–5).

The last family metaphor that I cite is Yahweh as Israel's *kinsman redeemer*. Recall that the duty of the *gōʾēl* was to redeem the family member (or the family property) who had been sold into slavery because of debts. Israel is that *impoverished kinsman* in need of a redeemer. If the judgment of God had sent his people into exile and resulted in the loss of their land, now Yahweh would redeem them with his mighty arm to bring them back (Isa. 41:14; 43:14; Jer. 50:34). Just as he had redeemed them many years before from bondage in Egypt, so once more he would liberate them from Babylon and other faraway places. The metaphor of Yahweh as a redeemer, like those of Yahweh as parent and husband, carries the expectation of spiritual and moral responsibility. This nation, which had enjoyed the blessing of redemption, was to be gracious and generous to the oppressed within its midst and redeem them from their heavy yoke of debt (Jer. 34:12–16).

These family metaphors also can occur in pairs. This fact underscores the theological and experiential reality that no one metaphor is adequate to describe the person of Yahweh. It also reinforces the warning about making too much of certain metaphorical language in order to offer generalizations about family life and the person of God. In each of these cases it is certain that one metaphor is juxtaposed with the other to highlight specific features or dimensions of Yahweh's character and activity that need to be held in tension to meet the needs of Israel in that context. Some of these pairs include Yahweh as father and husband to Israel (Jer. 3:4, 14, 19; Ezek. 16), as father and redeemer (Isa. 63:16), and as husband and redeemer (Isa. 54:5). Each of these passages describes his commitment to restore his people.

In summary, the Old Testament prophets offer a rich fund of images of Yahweh and his relationship with his people that find their basis in the extended family. These metaphors forcefully communicate the intensity and the enduring nature of the divine commitment, while at the same time emphasizing the mutuality of the relationship. God's people are to respond to him in respect, faithfulness, and obedience. This relationship is very personal and very passionate. We really do matter in the sight of Yahweh!

Conclusion

The Prophetic literature perhaps does not present as much direct information as we would like about the family. Nevertheless, there is more than what one might expect. The scenes that are brought to the reader's attention and the prophets' metaphors from the family are fraught with emotion. These passages do not allow for passive reading. Their rhetoric seeks a response and lets us know that questions about the family ultimately are inseparable from questions about God. To comprehend what is expected within family life allows us access into dimensions of our relationship with Yahweh; to know Yahweh truly, on the other hand, will educate and shape us for a better family life.

Although we are separated by many centuries from the world of the prophets, we yearn for much the same thing that they did: healthy families under God with the divine blessing. May we begin to mine the wealth of guidance within the prophetic message for the sake of our own families and the Christian church. May we appreciate in new ways how this revelation should be fundamental to our understanding of the significance of our adoption as sons and daughters by the heavenly father and to our anticipation of the glories of the wedding of the church, his bride, to the divine husband. At the same time, let us not forget that this relationship, expressed in so many wonderful ways, requires of us responsibilities that will honor and deepen that relationship. Those prophets of long ago serve as wise and deeply committed guides for that eternal pilgrimage.

PART 2

Family in the New Testament

6

Family in the Gospels and Acts

Cynthia Long Westfall

We usually do not go to the Gospels or Acts to build our theology of family. Among other things, there seems to be a confusion of signals. Did Jesus support family values,[1] or did he undermine the family?[2] Did he empower children and women,[3] or did he affirm patriarchy?[4] Did he teach responsibility toward family members,[5] or did he negate family duties?[6] The Gospels

---

1. See K. O. Gangel, "Toward a Biblical Theology of Marriage and Family, Part 3: Gospels and Acts," *JPsychTh* 5 (1977): 247–59: "All that God said of the family in the Old Testament is affirmed and reaffirmed in the New Testament with very few new concepts added" (247).

2. The theory that Jesus subverted the family and that family relationships meant little to him appears to have been suggested first by E. Renan, *The Life of Jesus* (New York: Modern Library, 1897), 97–98.

3. See E. Schüssler Fiorenza, *In Memory of Her* (Garden City, N.Y.: Doubleday, 1983). For a moderate example, see the discussion on gender roles in Luke-Acts in C. Osiek and D. L. Balch, *Families in the New Testament World: Households and House Churches* (Louisville: Westminster John Knox, 1997), 140–43. Osiek and Balch do not suggest an egalitarian model but do note how new ideals for gender relationships are established particularly in Luke.

4. See J. W. Pryor, "Jesus and Family—A Test Case," *ABR* 45 (1997): 56–69.

5. As Gangel purported (see n. 1), so that the picture in the Old Testament is enforced.

6. See D. C. Sim, "What about the Wives and Children of the Disciples? The Cost of Discipleship from Another Perspective," *HeyJ* 35 (1994): 373–90.

have been used to support all of these positions. A synthesis of Jesus' teachings about family relationships, his actions toward family groups, and his relationship with his own family helps us to navigate a maze of seemingly conflicting evidence. Although Jesus strengthened the family, he prioritized the kingdom of God and his mission above the family.

Jesus Strengthened the Family

Jesus explicitly strengthened the family through teaching. He valued children highly: he made himself accessible to them, blessed them, and portrayed them as his representatives as well as models of faith and humility (Matt. 18:1–5; 19:13–15; Mark 9:33–37; Luke 9:46–48; 18:15–17). Here he reinforced the command to honor parents and condemned the tradition of *corban*, which provided a loophole against providing for elderly parents (Mark 7:9–13). He strengthened a commitment to fidelity in marriage as well as monogamy. He strengthened the Old Testament's commands against adultery by claiming that even lust was adultery (Matt. 5:27–28). He went beyond the law and forbade the practice of divorce (allowed by the Mosaic law) and characterized it as a form of adultery (Matt. 5:31–32; 19:1–9; Mark 10:1–12; Luke 16:18).

It is important to note that in strengthening the family Jesus was more of a prophetic voice that confronted the contemporary religious views and challenged traditional emphases. Furthermore, when Christianity spread to the Gentiles, Jesus' teaching on children, adultery, divorce, and monogamy had a more radical impact on the Greco-Roman family than it had on Jewish culture. The Christian ethic included Jesus' teaching, and it also carried over specific Judaic injunctions against incest, infanticide, and abortion.

The Value and Importance of Children

Jesus stressed the importance and value of children. It was traditional in the Jewish culture to value children. Children were a blessing from the Lord,[7] and producing children was an

7. Since the Jewish identity involved being a covenant people and a "holy race" (Ezra 9:2), children were seen as a blessing to the family and an insurance of the nation's perpetuity. See D. L. Stamps, "Children in Late Antiquity," *DNTB*, 197–201.

act of obedience to the biblical mandate in Gen. 1:28 to "be fruitful and multiply." However, the fact that children were valued did not mean that they were regarded as important in the sense that they had status in the Jewish culture. Jesus used a child as an example of one who had status in the kingdom because children had no status or importance—a child was the ultimate example of humility (Matt. 18:1–5; Mark 9:33–37; Luke 9:46–48).[8] The disciples tried to prevent children from coming to Jesus because they believed that a rabbi was too important to be interrupted by interaction with children (Matt. 19:13–15; Luke 18:15–17).[9] It was unusual for a rabbi to give children precedence or to elevate them as models of humility and faith, let alone single them out as his personal representatives. Jesus' use of children as an identity for his disciples and an example of faith stands in contrast with both the traditional Jewish culture and the Epistles, which describe childhood as a time of immaturity, discipline, or unrealized potential.[10]

8. D. A. Hagner (*Matthew 14–28*, WBC 33B [Dallas: Word, 1995], 517) states, "The social insignificance, if not the innocent unself-consciousness of the little child, was the very antithesis of the disciples' interest in power and greatness." C. Keener (*A Commentary on the Gospel of Matthew* [Grand Rapids: Eerdmans, 1999], 448) comments, "Perhaps due to the high infant mortality rate among rural peasants, ancient Mediterranean parents sometimes may have been slower than are their modern Western counterparts to attach themselves too deeply to their younger children. Yet disciples must imitate such people of no status, people who recognize their dependence." See also C. Blomberg, *Matthew*, NAC (Nashville: Broadman, 1992), 272–74.

9. According to A. Verhey (*The Great Reversal: Ethics and the New Testament* [Grand Rapids: Eerdmans, 1984], 20), "Forbid them not, for of such is the kingdom of God (Mark 10:14) is a concrete command that challenges both conventional expectations of the kingdom and the customary rules of pomp, protocol, and behavior." Keener (*Matthew*, 473) adds, "Children were low-status dependents; they had to trust adults and receive what they provided. . . . Low in status, they could not be permitted to deter a teacher like Jesus from 'important' matters—at least, this was the view of the disciples." See also Blomberg, *Matthew*, 294–96.

10. Stamps ("Children in Late Antiquity," 200–201) says, "In the epistles there is the general perspective that a child represents a stage of development that one is to grow out of (i.e., immaturity) or a state of being that is unrealized potential (1 Cor. 13:11; 14:20; James 1:6; Heb. 5:13; 1 Peter 2:2). In the Gospels children represent an identity to which disciples should aspire and from which disciples learn (Matt. 18:1–5; Mark 9:33–37; 10:13–16). The difference between Jesus' teaching and the epistles is an interesting point of theological and historical reflection."

128   Family in the New Testament

The value and importance that Jesus placed on children stands
in even greater contrast with the Greco-Roman culture. Theoretically, children were seen as part of the kinship tradition and carri-
ers of the family name and business. In reality, children had low
status and no power in society, and infants often were treated as
expendable.[11] The widespread practice of abortion and infanticide
resulted in a birthrate so low that the population was declining.[12]
The decline in birthrate was aggravated by the fact that infanticide
or abandonment was more often practiced on female infants at
the command of the father for economic reasons.[13] Because of the
ban on abortion and infanticide, early Christian practice naturally
produced not only more children but also a larger ratio of women
to men than was current in the Roman Empire.[14] The early
church's application of the value and importance of children had
an unexpected sociological and demographic impact, particularly
as the church grew exponentially.

11. Children represented the bottom of the social and economic scale. T. F.
Carney observes, "Age divisions, and commensurate power and responsibility,
were hierarchical, sharply demarcated and significant. Authority ran vertically
downwards. Age and tradition were revered and powerful" (*The Shape of the
Past: Models and Antiquity* [Lawrence, Kans.: Coronado, 1975], 92).
12. R. Stark, *The Rise of Christianity: How the Obscure, Marginal Jesus
Movement Became the Dominant Religious Force in the Western World in a Few
Centuries* (San Francisco: HarperSanFrancisco, 1997), 115–17.
13. Traditionally, when a woman was married, she belonged to her husband's family; consequently, both Jews and Gentiles preferred sons. N. Lewis
quotes a letter from an absent husband who instructs his wife: "If you are delivered of a child [before I come home], if it is a boy keep it, if a girl discard it"
(*Life in Egypt under Roman Rule* [Oxford: Clarendon, 1985], 54). D. L. Stamps
describes the Roman custom of setting a newborn on the ground in front of the
father for him to inspect. If the father lifted up the child, it symbolized the newborn's acceptance into the family. If the father left the baby on the ground, it
symbolized that the child should be exposed ("Children in Late Antiquity,"
197–98). The Twelve Tables, the earliest Roman code, gave fathers the right to
practice infanticide. See also the discussion in C. Keener, "Family and Household," *DNTB*, 353–68, esp. 359–60.
14. According to Stark (*Rise of Christianity*, 97, 128), the Greco-Roman
world had an acute shortage of women. One estimate states that there were
140 males per 100 females in Italy, Asia Minor, and North Africa. Stark suggests, "Christian subcultures in the ancient world rapidly developed a very substantial surplus of females, while in the pagan world around them males
greatly outnumbered females. This shift was the result of Christian prohibi-
tions against infanticide and abortion and substantial sex bias in conversion."

Honoring Parents

Jesus' support of the command to honor one's father and mother reinforced strong traditional values shared by Jewish and Gentile cultures. However, his application clearly attacked an aspect of Jewish tradition when he said, "You have a fine way of setting aside the commands of God in order to observe your own traditions!" (see Mark 7:9–13). He condemned the contemporary Jewish practice of *corban,* in which a son superficially placed God first by dedicating all of his assets to God so that it was impossible to support his parents.[15] The practice allowed a son to keep all his money to himself. Thus, Jesus' teaching exposed the hypocritical use of religion against the family for selfish purposes as an example of how honoring the oral tradition concerning vows negated the commands of God.

Lust and Adultery

Jesus' indictment of lust (Matt. 5:27–30) may not have been more rigorous than what the rabbis and Pharisees taught. It was an application of the tenth commandment, "You shall not covet" (Exod. 20:17), to sexual behavior. Jesus equates its violation with breaking the seventh commandment, "You shall not commit adultery" (Exod. 20:14). The primary difference with Jesus' approach to lust is that Jesus placed the responsibility for lust completely on the person who is lusting. Jewish culture placed the bulk of the responsibility for adultery on women because they were held responsible for inciting lust.[16] For example, C. Keener observes, "Jewish people regarded a woman's premarital sexual activity as equivalent to prostitu-

15. W. L. Lane (*The Gospel of Mark,* NICNT [Grand Rapids: Eerdmans, 1974], 251) states, "If the son declared his property *corban* to his parents, he neither promised it to the Temple nor prohibited its use to himself, but he legally excluded his parents from the right of benefit. Should the son regret his action and seek to alleviate the harsh vow which would deprive his parents of all the help they might normally expect from him, he would be told by the scribes to whose arbitration the case was submitted that his vow was valid and must be honored."

16. Keener (*Matthew,* 187) writes, "Jewish men expected married Jewish women to wear head coverings to prevent lust (single women were exempt, since they needed to find a husband). Jewish writers often warned of women as dangerous because they could invite lust."

tion."[17] This assumption may explain why the woman who was caught in adultery in John 7:53–8:11 was confronted alone.[18] Although Jesus must have meant the prohibition against lust to be gender inclusive, it is clear by the masculine orientation that men were targeted at least as much as women in his command.

As Christianity spread to the Gentile culture, the countercultural impact of Jesus' condemnation of lust and adultery was much greater. In sexual matters, the Gentile society was characterized by a double standard in expectations, law, and practice. There were many socially accepted avenues for a man to engage in premarital sex, but an unmarried woman was expected to remain a virgin.[19] After marriage, a man's sexual relations with multiple unmarried women were not viewed as seriously as a married woman's adultery.[20] Early Christianity, on the other hand, was ethically egalitarian. R. Stark writes, "Like pagans, early Christians prized female chastity, but unlike pagans they rejected the double standard that gave pagan men so much sexual license. Christian men were urged to remain virgins until marriage, and extramarital sex was condemned as adultery."[21] With Christianity, a new standard of family values emerged that placed greater restrictions on the sexual behavior of husbands and fathers than was common in either Palestine or the Greco-Roman culture, so that the expectation and standards of faithfulness and trust between husbands and wives was reciprocal.

Divorce

Jesus' commands against divorce (Matt. 5:31–32; 19:1–9; Mark 10:1–12; Luke 16:18) were radical and unexpected, as evidenced by

17. C. Keener, "Adultery, Divorce," *DNTB*, 10.

18. Though the earliest and most reliable manuscripts do not include John 7:53–8:11, there is no reason to doubt that it constituted part of the oral tradition before it was included.

19. Keener, "Adultery, Divorce," 10.

20. Keener (ibid., 9) writes, "Honorable Roman men could sleep with unmarried women provided they were not of honorable lineage, but aristocratic Roman women could sleep only with their husbands." He continues, "The double standard also applied to the way historians evaluated their traditions; although monogamy was the norm, a man's multiple sexual relations with unmarried women were seen as far less serious than a married woman's infidelities because adultery was specifically a matter of stealing the wife's affections."

21. Stark, *Rise of Christianity*, 104.

the incredulous reactions of both the Pharisees and Jesus' own disciples. It was clear that Moses had allowed and regulated divorce in Deut. 24:1–4. In Palestine, divorce was a man's prerogative; he could divorce a woman for "any and every reason."[22] In most of Palestine, a woman could not initiate a divorce except under extreme circumstances, where the court would intervene on her behalf.[23] While Jesus' statement is similar to some Pharisees' position in preventing divorce except in cases of immorality, Jesus is unique in shifting the emphasis to the point of view of the woman.[24] In Matt. 19:1–9, Jesus not only makes divorce equivalent to adultery but also suggests that it should not occur for the sake of the wife, who is portrayed as victimized by divorce.[25] Jesus' appeal to Gen. 2:24 also implied monogamy, which was another cornerstone of the Christian ethic. The disciples are repelled by the prospect of an unending monogamous relationship and counter with the retort "If that is the relationship of a man with his wife, it is better not to marry!" Divorce was common in the Roman Empire. However, opposition to divorce and the ideal of an enduring monogamous relationship became a core value of the Christian ethic.

22. Keener ("Adultery, Divorce," 6) states, "Palestinian Jewish husbands could divorce for virtually any reason (though this is not to imply that the average husband was looking for excuses to divorce his wife)."

23. Ibid.

24. A. E. Harvey (*Strenuous Commands: The Ethic of Jesus* [London: SCM, 1990], 88) comments, "But just as we found that Jesus' beatitudes often differ from those in the wisdom tradition by being directed towards the poor and disadvantaged, so his maxim on divorce is distinctive in virtue of its concern for the wife as much as for the husband. The law on adultery was strictly egalitarian: the adulterer and the adulteress were to receive equal punishment. By making divorce equivalent to adultery, Jesus seems to have brought this equal treatment into the sphere of marriage. 'He who divorces his wife makes *her* the victim of adultery' (Matt. 5.31). The implied reason is that it is for the sake of the wife that divorce should be abjured. If Jesus is using a wisdom form to express a wisdom-type maxim, he has once again shifted the traditional emphasis from the stronger to the weaker, from the man to the woman. In the wisdom tradition this is unprecedented; and it is notably absent even from early Christian reflection on the subject, which consistently adopts the point of view of the male."

25. In analyzing Matt. 19:3–12, Osiek and Balch (*Families*, 132) claim, "The debate is androcentric and patriarchal, focused on what a husband may do (v. 3)." However, the androcentricity reflects the Palestinian practice, because it is generally agreed that as a rule, women in Palestine did not initiate divorce. The concern about forcing a woman involved in a divorce to be an adulteress is not a patriarchal concern.

Wives and Mothers

The Christian ethic directly impacted the quality of life for wives and mothers. Infidelity, polygamy, divorce, incest, infanticide, and abortion devalued and destroyed women.[26] Abortion by poison and mechanical methods were common forms of birth control that were a major cause of female death and infertility.[27] Consequently, under the Christian ethic, women enjoyed far greater marital security, safety, and equality than did their pagan counterparts. R. Stark proposes that the higher status of women in Christianity was a prime factor in the conversion ratios in the Roman Empire. Women converts to Christianity far exceeded men, even though there was a shortage of women in the Roman Empire.[28] By sanctifying marriage and making equal demands in fidelity, Christian teachings cut across destructive prerogatives of privilege in a culture that marginalized women and marriage.[29]

Father-Son Terminology

Jesus showed an appreciation of the strength of family bonds by using family terminology to describe roles and relationships

26. Infidelity, polygamy, incest, and infanticide were problems inherent in the ancient patriarchal system. Osiek and Balch (*Families*, 56) observe, "In the family, the legal and social power of father over wife, children, slaves, and property was extensive in all the ancient Mediterranean societies known to us." As Osiek and Balch note, "Men blamed women for having abortions, but then themselves exposed their children" (ibid., 65). Certainly, women initiated abortions to conceal illicit sexual activity. However, Stark (*Rise of Christianity*, 120) contends, "The very high rates of abortion in the Greco-Roman world can only be fully understood if we recognize that in perhaps the majority of instances it was men, rather than women, who made the decision to abort. Roman law accorded the male head of the family the literal power of life and death over his household, including the right to order a female in the household to abort."
27. For a description of methods of abortion, see Stark, *Rise of Christianity*, 119–21. Stark asserts, "Abortion not only prevented many births, it killed many women before they could make their contribution to fertility, and it resulted in a substantial incidence of infertility in women who survived abortion" (119).
28. See ibid., 122. J. C. Russell (*Late Ancient and Medieval Population* [Philadelphia: American Philosophical Society, 1958], 14) estimated that the imbalance of 140 men to every 100 women in Rome was a result of "some tampering with human life."
29. Some suggest that the cause of the decline in population came primarily from the male mentality that bachelorhood and childlessness were advantageous. See Osiek and Balch, *Families*, 65–66.

in the kingdom of God.[30] Jesus referred to God as his father and to himself as God's only, unique son (John 3:16). His claim of sonship and unity with God was taken as a claim of equality with God and of deity by the Jews (10:25–33). However, he also taught his followers to refer to God as their father and called them God's children (Matt. 6:9; 17:25–27). Jesus drew parallels between God's generosity, love, and forgiveness and that of human parents who know how to give good gifts to their children and welcome erring children back home as in the parable of the Prodigal Son (Luke 11:11–13; 15:11–32). The metaphor was extended so that believers were Jesus' brothers, sisters, and mother (Mark 3:31–35; Luke 8:19–21). The qualities stressed by the father-son relationship are identity, love, and nurture.[31] Readers were expected to transfer their positive patriarchal concepts about fathers to God. The connection of paternal authority with God and the designation of all believers as siblings had an equalizing effect on Jesus' followers. Jesus told his followers not to call anyone on earth either father or rabbi because they are all siblings and only God is their father and their master (Matt. 23:8–10). In an analysis of Mark 10:29–30, Osiek and Balch conclude, "The old family included a patriarchal father; the new one does not, since God is the only Father."[32]

30. The entire issue of *Semeia* 85 (1999) is concerned with the topic of "God the Father in the Gospel of John." K. O. Gangel lists a total of thirteen indications of family terminology in the New Testament. See Gangel, "Toward a Biblical Theology of Marriage and Family," 247–59, esp. 251–52.

31. Some take this use of terminology as an implicit ratification of the ancient patriarchal system. Pryor ("Jesus and Family," 62) asserts, "While Jesus does not exactly parade around proclaiming, 'I support the traditional family; I support patriarchy,' he nonetheless uses them as models in his teaching in such a way, and to such an extent, that would have been impossible for him had he actually believed otherwise about their validity." However, Jesus' teaching and behavior diminished androcentricity. Furthermore, Jesus' pervasive use of language about king and kingdom has not convinced us of a similar timeless validation of monarchy. Neither has the extensive use of slavery as a model in New Testament teaching convinced us of the timeless legitimacy of slavery as an institution.

32. Osiek and Balch, *Families*, 127. Contra Pryor ("Jesus and Family," 67), who maintains, "The fact that Jesus fails to mention fathers in the 'kingdom family,' far from denigrating the father role elevates it, for the heavenly Father becomes the pattern of all human fatherhood."

Jesus Strengthened the Family and Critiqued Tradition

Therefore, Jesus strengthened the family through teaching nurture, personal responsibility, inside-out faithfulness, and commitment. His use of family terminology for the kingdom of God demonstrates that the nature of the family corresponds to spiritual relationships within God's kingdom. Rather than validate the ancient patriarchal system, Jesus' sayings and commands that strengthened the family equalized relationships ethically and commended humility as opposed to operating from a posture of power and status. It would go too far to say that Jesus advocated egalitarianism, but his teaching cut across several prerogatives of the ancient patriarchal system that were destructive to the marriage relationship and the family members. The household of God was called to a higher standard with transformed identities, but believers were also called to function day to day within the contemporary social and political framework.

Jesus Relativized the Family

We must not forget that the focus of Jesus' teaching was on the kingdom of God, not the family. When Jesus chose his disciples and taught them and the crowds about discipleship, he relativized the priority of family without being antifamily.[33] Contemporary attacks and early Christian literature demonstrate that this relativization was perceived as undermining traditional family authority structure. J. Barclay asserts,

33. For precedents of the relativization of family ties in Philo, Josephus, the Cynics, and the Stoics, see S. C. Barton, *Discipleship and Family Ties in Mark and Matthew*, Society for New Testament Studies Monograph Series 80 (Cambridge: Cambridge University Press, 1994), 23–56; see also idem, "The Relativisation of Family Ties in the Jewish and Graeco-Roman Traditions," in *Constructing Early Christian Families: Family as Social Reality and Metaphor*, ed. H. Moxnes (London: Routledge, 1997), 81–100. Osiek and Balch (*Families*, 124–25) also present three contemporary examples from Roman, Greek, and Jewish texts to show that other ultimate values in these cultures relativized family values. They characterized Q similarly: "Like the Roman, Greek and Jewish texts, Q relativizes family without being antifamily" (126).

The practical effect of the early Christian movement was not to solidify but tó undermine family loyalties for a significant proportion of its adherents. Whatever partial parallels there may be outside Christianity to the notion that God (or philosophy) might take precedence over family ties, the fact remains that early Christianity became distinguished by this characteristic, whose importance led to a fundamental reconsideration of the worth of family loyalties and of the family as such.[34]

Yet R. Stark argues that the basis of the growth of early Christianity was through social networks, "through a structure of direct and intimate interpersonal attachments."[35] Family ties were one of the primary avenues of conversion. However, the initial family member to convert was often a woman or "child" under parental authority, so that the independent decision to convert was perceived as undermining family authority, unity, and values. Furthermore, the relatively high ratio of women to men in the church led to the intermarriage of Christian women with pagan men, resulting in Christian offspring as well as many "secondary" conversions of the head of the household.[36] Jesus' teaching and personal history demonstrate both the displacement of the family and the growth of the church through family ties.

The Priority of Discipleship

Jesus made it clear that discipleship needed to be a higher priority than family ties.[37] He predicted that he would disrupt

34. J. M. G. Barclay, "The Family as the Bearer of Religion in Judaism and Early Christianity," in *Constructing Early Christian Families,* ed. Moxnes, 74.

35. Stark, *Rise of Christianity,* 20.

36. Ibid., 95, 128. This pattern of conversion through wives and mothers would scarcely find favor with the opponents of Christianity or the proponents of ancient patriarchy.

37. Contra I. Ellis, "Jesus and the Subversive Family," *SJT* 38 (1985): 173–88. Ellis states, "He was not an 'enemy of the family' nor did he defend it, if both points of view failed to take into account the coming reign of God which he proclaimed. He operates on another plane entirely. He may be a more radical critic of the family as it has evolved in this-worldly mundane terms, and yet we have an altogether more sympathetic understanding of the human relationships which it embodies" (177). Jesus did not treat the kingdom of God as if it were on a different plane from the family. The family was treated as subject to God's ethics, a potential competitor for one's loyalties, and a vehicle for kingdom expansion.

the family and set family members against one another, and
said that if his followers loved family members more than him,
they were not worthy of him (Matt. 10:34–37). In Luke 14:26, he
uses hyperbole and asserts, "If anyone comes to me and does
not hate his father and mother, his wife and children, his brothers and sisters—yes, even his own life—he cannot be my disciple" (NIV). As R. Clapp notes, "Allegiance to the kingdom *pre-
cedes* the family."[38] Clapp also suggests that Jesus decentered
and relativized the family—the family is displaced—it cannot
be considered God's most important institution on earth. The
first priority of every believer is to follow Jesus' call. Families
can have expectations and demands that make obedience impossible. When they are denied, hostility and misunderstand-
ings will abound (Mark 13:9–13).[39] Our definitions of family responsibility, submission, and obedience among the spouses
and children must make room for direct obedience to God.

The Priority of Kingdom Relationships

Kingdom relationships are depicted as the believer's primary
family. The use of family terminology to describe kingdom relationships serves as a double-edged sword to family values.
When your own family does not believe, you must become
more bonded and committed to your spiritual family. When a
woman in a crowd said that Jesus' mother was blessed for giving birth to him and nursing him, he retorted that it was far
more important to obey God's word (Luke 11:27–28). He also
taught that people who do God's will are more of a family than
biological families who disobey God (Mark 3:31–35).[40] He even
taught his followers to invite the poor, crippled, lame, and blind

38. R. Clapp, *Families at the Crossroads: Beyond Traditional and Modern Options* (Downers Grove, Ill.: InterVarsity, 1993), 77.
39. In discussing Mark 13:9–13, Osiek and Balch (*Families*, 128) state, "Disciples are being betrayed 'to death' by their own families. And 13:13a is the only
time the verb 'hate' occurs in Mark. We begin to understand the commitments
and experiences that led to relativizing the old households, replaced by the new
eschatological family of Jesus."
40. According to Barton (*Discipleship and Family Ties*, 74), "The climactic
saying in [Mark] 3:35 which identifies the true, spiritual family of Jesus paves
the way for both Jesus' rejection by his natural kin and Jesus' teaching that discipleship would be likely to cost his followers their ties of natural kin as well."

to lunch or dinner instead of their own friends and relatives (Luke 14:12–14).

Employment and Household Economics

Both Jesus and his disciples left their family businesses in a culture that expected sons to learn their fathers' trades and to take over the businesses. Jesus left the carpenter's trade, Simon and Andrew left their nets (Mark 1:16–18), and James and John literally left their father in the boat (Mark 1:19–20). In leaving their occupations, they walked away from both security and their families' expectations, because the times were extraordinary. Jesus' parable of the Prodigal Son exemplifies a more extreme reversal of values concerning family property (Luke 15:11–32). Osiek and Balch suggest that the father's challenge to the older son to celebrate the return of the profligate brother breaks through and contradicts the values of the traditional agrarian economy:

> In ancient agrarian society, this challenge would be an alienating, offensive, implausible, potentially transforming metaphor of the kingdom of God clashing with centuries of domestic, didactic wisdom. The goal of the household is to increase property, against which the younger son sins. By its extravagant ending, Jesus' parable collides with this ordered world and evokes the protest of the elder brother.[41]

According to Jesus, the kingdom of God prioritized forgiveness and reconciliation over protecting the economic goals of the household.

Homelessness

During the years that the disciples traveled with Jesus, they were homeless by choice. When a scribe volunteered to follow him, Jesus warned him that it would involve being homeless: "Foxes have holes, and birds of the air have nests; but the Son of Man has nowhere to lay his head" (Matt. 8:19–20). When disciples were sent out to preach about the kingdom, part of the

41. Osiek and Balch, Families, 139–40.

commission was to take no food or money and little clothing (Mark 6:8–9; Matt. 10:9–10; Luke 9:3; 10:4). They were supported by charity, such as what was given by the women who supported them financially (Luke 8:1–3). Being itinerant was definitely not a traditional value, but the method suited the mission.

Family Duties

Although Jesus reinforced the Old Testament command to honor parents, at times he appeared to negate family duties. As Osiek and Balch note, "Disciples leave ordinary ties because the time is extraordinary, eschatological."[42] When a disciple asked permission to go and bury his father, Jesus replied, "Let the dead bury the dead" (Matt. 8:21–22; Luke 9:59–60). He also denied permission to another disciple who wanted to go back and say good-bye to his family (Luke 9:61–62). Osiek and Balch state,

> The eschatological crisis meant that persons faced choices about what is most fundamental in life, an ultimate demand more important than family. Parents in a patriarchal society experienced the anarchy of sons, daughters and daughters-in-law in the crisis of God's coming rule.[43]

What may be more disturbing is the evidence that Peter, and possibly others, left a wife and children to follow Jesus. Peter said to Jesus, "We have left everything to follow you!" and Jesus answered, "No one who has left home or brothers or sisters or mother or father or children or fields for me and the gospel will fail to receive a hundred times as much in this present age" (Mark 10:28–30 NIV). Since we know that Peter had a mother-in-law (Matt. 8:14), it is reasonable to assume that the references to children applied at least to him. It is clear that the cost of discipleship was partially paid by the disciples' families.[44] However, it also appears that at least some of the family mem-

42. Ibid., 126.
43. Ibid.
44. See Sim, "What about the Wives and Children," 373–90.

bers, such as Peter's mother-in-law and the mother of James and John, were supportive.

Singleness and Barrenness

For the Jewish culture, the mandate to procreate was in the law (Gen. 1:28). Children were seen as a blessing and the insurance of the nation's and the individual's perpetuity. A childless married woman was an object of pity, and she felt shame (1 Sam. 1:10–11; Luke 1:25). In this cultural context, Jesus himself was celibate, and he not only supported men in "becoming eunuchs for the sake of the kingdom" (Matt. 19:12) but also called barren and childless women blessed and warned pregnant women about impending disaster (Mark 13:17–19; Luke 23:28–30).[45] Most are agreed that these statements reflect an expectation of disaster or the apocalypse. Jesus' ministry took place in the context of a volatile sociopolitical milieu in first-century Palestine that eventually culminated in the destruction of Jerusalem and the temple as well as the disruption of the surrounding environs, including North Africa and Samaria. The context of the early church was equally volatile until the fourth century. Any pregnant or nursing women caught in the middle of a military uprising or a persecution would be in an extremely difficult situation. At least in an eschatological context, Jesus did not see a woman's primary identity and value as being a wife and mother.[46] Jesus' and Paul's support of celibacy (1 Cor. 7:8–38) contributed to the renunciation of marriage by some women, which caused serious conflict with family authorities.[47]

45. For further discussion, see B. J. Pitre, "Blessing the Barren and Warning the Fecund: Jesus' Message for Women concerning Pregnancy and Childbirth," *JSNT* 81 (2001): 59–80.

46. The support of celibacy and barrenness should not be read in contradiction to the marriage and fertility of Christian women referred to in the first section. Jesus' teaching led to both an increased birthrate and a parallel advocacy of celibacy.

47. There is evidence that a renunciation of marriage by women was encouraged and supported. Though we know that intermarriage with unbelievers occurred, it was frowned on by church authorities. In view of the skewed gender ratios in the church, these authorities may have preferred that women renounce marriage rather than marry unbelievers. See the *Acts of Paul and Thecla,* and Barton's discussion in *Discipleship and Family Ties,* 8–11.

Costly Religion and Family Ties

It is hard to reconcile how Jesus could strengthen the family and at the same time make strenuous demands on his disciples that create conflict with the family. However, a costly religion with high commitment is, paradoxically, very attractive to outside observers, including a convert's immediate family.[48] In spite of the fact that following Jesus caused conflict among families, Christianity spread primarily through attachments—friends and families. When the rest of the family chooses to follow Jesus, then the family has found its way home within kingdom relationships, and in that case the biological family truly becomes an integral part of the most important institution on earth.

Jesus' Family Ties

If Jesus truly had been a destroyer of the family relationship, and if those relationships had meant little to him, then it is doubtful that we would have found his immediate family praying with the disciples in the upper room between his crucifixion and Pentecost (Acts 1:14). Jesus' own experience with his family mirrors the difficulty of family ties, the ordeal of family displacement, and the development of kingdom relationships through family attachments. Jesus' family ties and childhood were not "normal" or "traditional." They were difficult and messy.

Mary the Unwed Mother

The circumstances of Jesus' birth show that through the incarnation, God truly was willing to get involved in the messiness of our lives.[49] When the angel Gabriel appeared to Mary and told her that she would conceive God's son as a virgin, she

48. Stark, *Rise of Christianity*, 3–27, 163–89, passim.
49. As E. R. Fraser (*Confessions of a Beginning Theologian* [Downers Grove, Ill.: InterVarsity, 1998], 32) observes, "God hasn't abandoned the messiness of our lives in favor of less threatening involvement in a world of ideas. As a theologian I'm called to reflect this engagement of God with human history."

immediately responded to the call without asking permission to talk with her fiancé or her parents. However, the miraculous nature of her pregnancy could not take away the stigma or existential shame of being a pregnant single woman. She was completely vulnerable and soon was threatened with divorce. (In Palestine, an engagement was considered to be binding, and one had to obtain a divorce to break the engagement.[50]) Jesus' nuclear family was off to a dysfunctional start.[51]

Joseph the Stepfather

Joseph justifiably felt dishonored by Mary's pregnancy.[52] His hand was forced, and nothing on earth could stop him from divorcing Mary.[53] He planned to divorce her quietly, but, of course, silence is no protection to a single woman in her third trimester in a village community. A divorce would have been disaster for both Mary and Jesus.[54] God sent an angel to call Joseph to what may have been a more difficult role than Mary's

50. See Keener, *Matthew*, 90–91.

51. For further consideration of Mary, see B. R. Gaventa, "A Place for Mary in Protestant Ministry?" *Word and World* 13, no. 4 (1993): 373–78. She suggests that Mary's story focuses on the "marginalized, those who live at the fringes of power and acceptability. Mary's existence on the margins, as reflected both in the scandal in Matthew's gospel and in Mary's poverty implicit in Luke's gospel, re-presents to the church the claims of those who continue to live on the margins" (375–76).

52. S. C. Barton asserts, "Honor and shame were pivotal social values and were related closely to gender definition. Women were a potential source of shame, and it was the role of the male household head to guard the family's honor by protecting the women's sexual virtue" ("Living as Families in the Light of the New Testament," *Int* 52 [1998]: 133). A broader context for the social values of honor and shame is provided in D. A. deSilva, "Honor and Shame," *DNTB*, 518–22.

53. Keener (*Matthew*, 91) observes, "In contrast to most of Western culture, Joseph lived in a society where he had no option of giving Mary a second chance even if he wanted to (which he presumably would not have). Jewish, Greek and Roman law all demanded that a man divorce his wife if she were guilty of adultery."

54. Gaventa ("Place for Mary," 375) states, "Even with the best intentions and the fewest words spoken in public, the action he contemplates leaves Mary pregnant and without a father for her child. In the world of the first century, the consequences for Mary and her child would be devastating. Only divine intervention in the form of a dream prevents the scandal from erupting."

call. He was asked to support and protect Mary and the child that was not his. The birth in the stable must have felt like total humiliation and failure on his part as the head of the family. However, he was responsive and obedient to God's warnings and took his small family to Egypt to prevent Jesus from being murdered. The last time we see Joseph is when he and Mary find Jesus in the temple talking with the elders at the age of twelve. Jesus asked, "Why were you searching for me? Didn't you know I had to be in my father's house?" (Luke 2:49 NIV). The Scripture says that Joseph and Mary did not understand what he was saying to them. But Joseph would have picked up one message that every stepfather hears at some point: "You aren't my father." He was a displaced father.

Jesus the Illegitimate Son

As for Jesus, it is likely that he grew up under a cloud of illegitimacy. In the Greco-Roman world, legitimacy was vitally important because of the laws of rights and inheritance.[55] In Judaism, lineage and inheritance were essential, especially for any messianic claims.[56] The genealogies are insights that the authors give to the Gospel readers but that family, friends, and neighbors lacked. Regardless of who was initially informed of Mary's pregnancy, all would have noticed that Jesus' birth was "too soon."[57] Rumors of Joseph's plans to divorce may have leaked out in a village with a small-town culture. It may be significant that after leaving Nazareth when Mary was pregnant, Joseph and Mary stayed away in Bethlehem until compelled to go to Egypt.

When returning from Egypt, Joseph tried first to stay in Judah, but ended up being divinely maneuvered back to Nazareth, where he and Mary had a past (Matt. 2:19–23; Luke 1:26–

55. See W. K. Lacey, *The Family in Classical Greece* (Ithaca, N.Y.: Cornell University Press, 1968), 30.

56. Keener (*Matthew*, 73) notes, "Matthew opens his Gospel by showing both Jesus' historic inseparability from the history of Israel and his inseparability from the Gentile mission already implicit in that history."

57. The Lukan narrative makes clear that Mary stayed with Elizabeth for three months after conceiving and that she and Joseph were still engaged when they took the trip to Bethlehem (Luke 1:56; 2:5).

27).[58] Therefore, though Jesus grew up in a safe environment with relatives and friends (Luke 2:44), he also was faced with the people who would have been the first to question his parentage—they thought they knew his business. Much later, during his ministry, Jesus has a heated interchange with a group of Jews about parentage. They finally protest, *"We* are not illegitimate children" (John 8:41), and some see that as a slander of Jesus' virgin birth. D. A. Carson writes,

> It is not at all impossible that the Jews are alluding to the irregularities connected with Jesus' birth. From their perspective, he displays considerable cheek to talk about paternity: *they* were not born of fornication (wink, wink).[59]

Jesus was "set up" from the time that he was a small child to experience this kind of painful innuendo. His childhood experiences were not traditional.

The Displacement of Jesus' Family

When Jesus started his ministry, his family soon became displaced. First, his neighbors in Nazareth amazed him with their unbelief, to which he replied, "Prophets are not without honor, except in their own hometown, and among their own kin, and in their own house" (Mark 6:1–6a NRSV).[60] His brothers did not follow him or believe in him. They tried to taunt him so that he would place himself in danger (John 7:1–9). Though Mary had been pondering the different events in Jesus' life and had witnessed the miracle at Cana, it appears that she went through a period of confusion. She accompanied her sons to where Jesus was teaching and tried to restrain him because they believed that he was having a nervous break-

58. Keener (*Matthew*, 112–13) stresses the political insignificance and divine significance of the divine choice of Nazareth. From Mary's standpoint, the choice would have had personal significance.

59. D. A. Carson, *The Gospel according to John,* Pillar Commentary (Leicester, Eng.: Inter-Varsity; Grand Rapids: Eerdmans, 1991), 352.

60. Barton (*Discipleship and Family Ties,* 95) cites the crisis in Jesus' hometown as "yet another episode in the life of Jesus the authoritative Son of God, in which his divine vocation sets him at odds with those to whom he is tied by kinship and cohabitation."

down.[61] At that point, when his family was outside, Jesus pointedly said that his family was the one inside, who did the will of God, implying that his family outside the door was not doing the will of God (Mark 3:20–21, 31–35).[62] When a woman in a crowd cried out, "Blessed is the womb that bore you and the breasts that nursed you!" (Luke 11:27 NRSV), Jesus' response was as much a warning to Mary as a correction to the woman. Mary had been called the "blessed one" at the annunciation, but in order to be blessed now, she had to hear the word of God and obey it.

Kingdom Recognition

By the time Jesus was nailed to the cross, Mary was in a stage of kingdom recognition. In contrast to others who stood against him or were clueless about where to stand, she stood at the foot of the cross (John 19:25).[63] At that time Jesus did something highly symbolic: he assigned Mary a new son (John 19:26–27). This was Jesus' sign that she had become fully "blessed" at perhaps the lowest point in her life. It was a sign that she was hearing the word of God and obeying it. Mary was the first one from Jesus' immediate family to convert.

61. C. Myers cites this episode as not only an indication of a rift between Jesus and his family but also a repudiation of the kinship system (*Binding the Strong Man: A Political Reading of Mark's Story of Jesus* [Maryknoll, N.Y.: Orbis, 1988], 167–68). Myers states that Jesus' family attempted to "seize" him, a word that Mark uses for political detainment (6:17; 12:12; 14:1, 44, 46, 49, 51). However, while this word is used for forceful action such as "arrest," it is also used for "holding on" to traditions or taking a child by the hand in the performance of a miracle. Probably in all occurrences, a forceful idea of grabbing or grasping is in view. Myers suggests that their real fear was that Jesus was courting disaster with the highest authorities in the land, and they wished to protect him as well as themselves.

62. Barton (*Discipleship and Family Ties*, 86) cites this episode in Mark 3:31–35 as a turning point: "The story of Jesus and his family expresses the evangelist's firm conviction that the basis of relations in the people of God has been reconstituted once and for all."

63. Gaventa ("Place for Mary," 378) comments, "In a sense, however, Mary's presence at the cross touches on a profound feature of Christian ministry. Unlike those who appear to be insiders (Judas, Peter), she has neither betrayed nor denied Jesus. Unlike those who appear to be powerful (Pilate, the Roman soldiers), she knows where to stand. Standing by, she watches what God is doing."

Shortly after the crucifixion but before Pentecost, Mary and Jesus' brothers were joining together with the believers constantly in prayer (Acts 1:14). At that point, Jesus' immediate family had also become his spiritual family. We know that his brother James became the most influential elder in the Jerusalem church (Acts 12:17; 15:14; 21:18) and is purported by tradition to be the author of the Book of James. Mary became an important source for Luke's Gospel, as she had "treasured all these things in her heart" (2:51 NRSV). The displacement of Jesus' family was not permanent, and the kingdom grew through Jesus' family ties.

Life in the Trenches

The Book of Proverbs is life from the royal point of view. When all things are equal, the principles in Proverbs work on the basis of cause and effect. However, the life of Jesus was located far from the royal road—it was life in the trenches. All things were not equal in Jesus' life. Mary was an unwed mother, he was raised in a blended family with a stepfather, and he grew up under a cloud of illegitimacy. His was a life of conflicting authorities, and he faced a crossfire of voices. He experienced opposition from those whom one would expect to be allies: his own family and the people who took religion seriously. Jesus' life is not a pattern for the traditional family; rather, he shows us how to be involved in, and navigate, the messiness of our lives.

Conclusion: Jesus and Family Values

Jesus' teachings on the family confronted cultural abuses and formed a basis for significant sociological change in the Greco-Roman world as the early church grew. The church's subsequent rejection of infidelity, polygamy, divorce, incest, infanticide, and abortion positively shaped the ethics of future societies. As a whole, his teachings were confrontational and cannot be characterized as affirming traditional patriarchal models; they moved the Christian model of the family to higher ground. It is interesting that we now face some of the same issues of infidelity, divorce, incest, and abortion. Individualism and self-actualization have become more important than marital commitment and the value of children. The early church demonstrated that Christianity can survive and grow in a pluralistic culture that faces these challenges. Even more, if lived and applied effectively and authentically, Christianity can still offer solutions to the acute problems that face society.

However, Jesus did not intend the family to be the most important institution on earth or the central unit of a Christian's identity and purpose.[64] He taught that kingdom relationships held a higher priority than family relationships and that his mission took precedence over familial demands and expectations. The necessity to prioritize a bond with God's people and to develop a sense of mission is the crying need of the postmodern Christian. But instead of a costly commitment to the kingdom, many believers are characterized by fragmentation, individualism, and a consumer mentality toward the church. One sometimes senses the conviction that the church exists to serve the family and to maintain the family's well-being. It is believed that the family must be guarded from overcommitment to the church. One hears that Sundays are family days and sometimes are better spent in the mountains in quality family time instead of in fellowship. Unless believers can recover an eschatological commitment to the church and the kingdom's mission, Christianity will not be able to provide the answers that will heal families and society.

Jesus' incarnation demonstrates how God works in and through our family ties. The circumstances of the incarnation blow apart stereotypes and utopian ideals of how God works through the family. Jesus belonged to a family that would be considered dysfunctional rather than ideal, particularly according to the contemporary culture's standards. He demonstrates that God breaks through and utilizes our imperfect cir-

64. Contra R. J. Rushdoony (*Salvation and Godly Rule* [Vallecito, Calif.: Ross House, 1983], 477): "The exercise of dominion over all creation of Gen. 1:28 is essential to the life of church, state, and school, to arts and sciences, to every calling and every phase of life, but, in its primary assignment and orientation, is given to the family. The central area of dominion is . . . the family under God."

cumstances to accomplish his purposes. He does not require a traditional family to qualify us for his kingdom or mission. He identifies with us in our broken places and heals them. Nevertheless, family ties can be an avenue of redemption and an opportunity for ministry for every individual.

7

Family in the Epistles

STANLEY E. PORTER

The family is one of the most vital concepts in contemporary Christian culture. It is recognized by professionals, such as counselors and clergy, and laity alike that the family is one of the most important—if not *the* most important—mainstays of our society. In the world in which we live, however, there is also much lamenting of the change of the traditional family. We are constantly reminded of the high incidence of divorce; the large number of single-parent families; the problem of latch-key kids; the debate over daycare; the issues of attention deficit disorder, food additives, and family responsibility; and a host of other problems. It is not only the church but also other institutions that warn of the family being under attack. Recent psychological studies, for example, have revived the long-debated question of how much damage divorce does to the children involved.

In light of the importance of the family, when I was first invited to make a contribution on the topic of the family in the New Testament Epistles, I all too gladly accepted. I have long been interested in the legal construction of the ancient Roman family, and this essay has given me a chance to indulge my interest, especially as it might have implications for understanding some of the crucial "familial" passages elsewhere in the New Testament.

The Predicament

An investigation of the family in the Epistles of the New Testament almost immediately encounters difficulties, however. The Greek word for "family" (πατριά, *patria*) is used three times in the New Testament, but only once in the Epistles, in Eph. 3:15 (see also Luke 2:4; Acts 3:25). In Eph. 3:14–15, Paul says, "For this cause I bow my knees unto the Father of our Lord Jesus Christ, of whom the whole family in heaven and earth is named." There is no other obvious single Greek word to consider, and even this one is clearly not the equivalent of what we understand as "family," but means something more like "social grouping."[1]

At this point, anyone considering the family in the Epistles is faced with several options. One option is to write a brief essay on a single verse, Eph. 3:15.[2] In such an essay, however, one could note several important things. One is that Paul has a very large view of God, acknowledging that the scope of his power extends throughout both heaven and earth. Paul says that God is the one who is responsible for having named every social grouping, here probably referring to tribes and nations of peoples, families in the sense of those descended from the same ancestor. A number of interpreters have tried to overly restrict the notion of the family to the church, but this is unlikely in this particular context. Some may wonder what such groups are in heaven. It may well be that Paul has in mind a number of different groups that populate heaven, such as angels, to all of which God has given names. Or it might be that Paul is using

---

1. See E. Best, *A Critical and Exegetical Commentary on Ephesians*, ICC (Edinburgh: Clark, 1998), 334.

2. A recent book on the theological notion of family does not even treat this verse in this light and mentions it only once in a footnote. See J. H. Hellerman, *The Ancient Church as Family* (Minneapolis: Fortress, 2001), 258. Hellerman restricts himself to "the documents that are universally assigned to Pauline authorship" (92).

"heaven and earth" in a contrastive sense to include the totality of created and named being. In the ancient world, the notion of naming has connotations of power and control over those named, and that is certainly present in this particular verse. These social groupings are presided over by a father, but not just any father. This father is the father God, who is creator and overseer of this cosmos. There is clearly a play on the word "father" (πατήρ, *patēr*) in the use of the word πατριά to describe those who are named by him, reinforcing the relation between the namer and the named.[3] This single verse has in fact quite a bit to say about the scope of God's encompassing power but not much to say about what we would usually think of when we consider the concept of family.

The Solution

Word Studies

As we noted, a simple word search arrives at minimal results in coming to an understanding of the family in the New Testament Epistles—a single reference in a book that many, if not most, New Testament scholars think was almost assuredly not written by Paul and may not even have been an epistle in the usual sense.[4] But then why should a single word be expected to do so much?

The word-study approach to New Testament exegesis has produced many unfortunate results. The tendency in New Testament exegesis has been to atomize the text of the New Testament and analyze it in word-by-word units. One can pick up almost any major commentary and find such exegesis as it proceeds word by word through the text. There is much information about each individual word, but unfortunately, in more instances than not, the sense of the text as a text is lost. What we

3. See A. Lincoln, *Ephesians*, WBC 42 (Waco, Tex.: Word, 1990), 42; Best, *Ephesians*, 338–39; M. Y. MacDonald, *Colossians and Ephesians*, SP 17 (Collegeville, Minn.: Liturgical Press, 2000), 275.
4. I do not hold to these views, but that is another essay. See L. M. McDonald and S. E. Porter, *Early Christianity and Its Sacred Literature* (Peabody, Mass.: Hendrickson, 2000), 482–87.

accumulate is a lot of what amounts to virtually worthless information about individual words. I use "virtually worthless" because the accumulation of data about a word almost assuredly could not all be brought to bear in the particular instance of usage. What is being exegeted by most New Testament interpreters is the accumulated meaning of the use of the word in its numerous and several New Testament contexts. The result is a theologizing of the individual words.

There is, of course, a distinct sense in which the entire New Testament is a theological book. However, this does not mean that each individual word is meant to bear the full weight of the accumulated theology and meanings of all other occurrences of the word in each single occurrence. Such a flaw is clearly seen in most of the theological dictionaries of the New Testament, especially G. Kittel and G. Friedrich's *Theological Dictionary of the New Testament*,[5] but numerous others as well. James Barr liked to call this (in his inelegant phrase) "illegitimate totality transfer," whereby all meanings are brought to bear when only one meaning is really accurate in the given context.[6] In other words, it is fortunate that there is no single word that is used for "family" in the Epistles, as this provides an opportunity to expand our understanding of the concept through a methodologically sounder procedure of examining, not just a particular word, but any word that is conceptually linked to the notion of family.

Semantic Domains

Semantic-domain theory provides a means of accessing such conceptually linked words. I am a firm and resolute user of the Louw-Nida semantic-domain lexicon of the Greek New Testament.[7] I consider this one of the greatest innovations and developments in linguistics in the twentieth century. I realize that there are many criticisms of this tool, including the fact that it was supposedly developed only for translators (which of us is

5. Trans. and ed. G. W. Bromiley, 10 vols. (Grand Rapids: Eerdmans, 1964–76).

6. J. Barr, *The Semantics of Biblical Language* (Oxford: Oxford University Press, 1961), 218.

7. J. P. Louw and E. A. Nida, *A Greek-English Lexicon Based on Semantic Domains*, 2 vols. (New York: American Bible Society, 1988).

not a translator of the Greek New Testament, since none of us is a native speaker of ancient Greek?), or that it limits its treatment to the Greek of the New Testament (again, it at least draws defensible boundaries to its corpus).[8] However, despite these ostensible shortcomings, the lexicon is a huge intellectual accomplishment in which one Greek dialect has been analyzed and lexicographicalized into its respective semantic domains.

Semantic-domain theory is very important for the study of the lexicon of a language. It works from the premise that we know words according to the semantic space that they occupy in our language usage. Therefore, words that are used for parts of the body, or colors, or clothing, or foods, for example, are related to each other in a way that words in an alphabetical list are not. As evidence that this is how we know words, one can think of all the words one knows and try to say them in alphabetical order, starting with *A*. It is impossible. But it is not impossible to start naming all the words one knows for colors, parts of the car, or body parts, for example.

In the Louw-Nida lexicon,[9] the domain in which πατριά appears is domain 10, "Kinship Terms," subdomain B, "Kinship Relations Involving Successive Generations," and entry 24. Entry 24 includes two words besides πατριά. These are οἶκος (*oikos*) and γένεσις (*genesis*). Γένεσις is used five times in the New Testament, but the two instances in the Epistles, James 1:23 and 3:6, are not used in the sense of "family." However, there are several useful instances of οἶκος, which often is translated "house." Many of these instances simply refer to a physical building (Rom. 16:5; 1 Cor. 11:34; 14:35; 16:19; Col. 4:15; Philem. 2; Heb. 3:3, 4; 1 Pet. 2:5). Other instances include 1 Cor. 1:16; 1 Tim. 3:4, 5, 12; 5:4; 2 Tim. 1:16; 4:19; Titus 1:11; Heb. 3:2, 5, 6; 8:8 (where family is extended to a tribe or lineage), 10 (where house and tribe are equated); 10:21; 11:7; and 1 Pet. 4:17. What is noteworthy in many if not most of these instances is that the term "house," which can refer to a physical

8. See S. E. Porter, *Studies in the Greek New Testament*, SBG 6 (New York: Peter Lang, 1996), 49–74.

9. The major structural principle of the lexicon is the division of the vocabulary of the Greek New Testament into ninety-three domains, or fields, of meaning, most of which have subdomains and individual entries with one or more lexical items (words).

structure, is metaphorically extended to refer to those who live in the house, and thus understood as a household, and even to include an entire tribe as if they were a group that lived together in a house. Similarly, another term often translated "house," οἰκία (*oikia*; 1 Cor. 11:22; 1 Tim. 5:13; 2 Tim. 2:20; 3:6; 2 John 10), is used in 1 Cor. 16:15; 2 Cor. 5:1 (2x); and Phil. 4:22, where the literal house comes to represent the household and its inhabitants. The term οἰκεῖος (*oikeios*), often translated "household," is a cognate form of οἶκος and is used in significant instances in all three of its occurrences. These are Gal. 6:10; Eph. 2:19; and 1 Tim. 5:8, where the literal sense of belonging to the household comes to represent the inhabitants of the house, who thereby belong to the same family. Galatians 6:10 speaks of the household of faith, and Eph. 2:19 of the household of God.[10]

There are a few preliminary conclusions that one can draw about the family in the Epistles from this brief survey of the words in the same semantic domain and their cognate terms. First, there is no single term for "family" in ancient Greek, especially in relation to what we think of today as a family, with a parent or two and 2.5 children.[11] Second, there is a mix of literal and figurative usage of the several words involved.[12] The literal words for a physical structure, a house, often are used metonymically for all that is contained within it—that is, the inhabitants of the house, its family. Third, this language itself is used with varying degrees of literalness and figurativeness. The household can be a literal family, such as would dwell in a particular house, but it can also be a house in relation to God, such as the uses of οἰκεῖος indicate in speaking of the household of faith or the household of God. This is a structure that is dedicated to, owned by, and operated by God and organized under his control, in which he is the head of the household.

10. On the first-century household, see S. Guijarro, "The Family in First-Century Galilee," in *Constructing Early Christian Families: Family as Social Reality and Metaphor*, ed. H. Moxnes (London: Routledge, 1997), 42–65.

11. H. Moxnes, "What Is Family? Problems in Constructing Early Christian Families," in *Constructing Early Christian Families*, ed. Moxnes, 13–41, esp. 20.

12. On metaphor regarding language of family, see E. M. Lassen, "The Roman Family: Ideal and Metaphor," in *Constructing Early Christian Families*, ed. Moxnes, 103–20, esp. 103–4.

What once seemed like a limited body of evidence clearly has expanded to some degree. What appears to be the case is that "house" language is transferred from a literalness to a metaphorical conception that can be used to speak figuratively of the occupants of a household all the way to a spiritual union that would, in some way, represent a family. The semantic subdomain thus has taken us an important step of the way in expanding our category of "family" language, allowing us to see that the metaphorical sense of the language is important to describe an entity that extends beyond simply literal boundaries.

Roman Law, the Family, and Kinship Terms

In order to know the outer limits of these boundaries, I think that it is necessary to try to understand what others besides the New Testament writers thought regarding the family. As Nicholas says in his summary of Roman law regarding the Roman family,

> In the early law, and to a considerable extent throughout Roman history, the family is the legal unit. Its head, the *paterfamilias*, is the only full person known to the law. His children, of whatever age, though they are citizens and therefore have rights in public law, are subject to his unfettered power of life and death. Again, only he can own property, and anything which his children acquire belongs to him alone. . . . In early law there was evidently little difference between son and slave, both being regarded as the property of the *paterfamilias* to be disposed of as he wishes.[13]

This concise definition essentially opens up all of the *kinship* terms to being *family* terms. Therefore, potentially at least, words for "father," "mother," "brother," "sister," "son," "daughter," "child," "firstborn," and even "grandmother" and "cousin" are family words. This is not surprising. What is perhaps more unusual is to think that terms such as "slave," "servant," "bastard," and "orphan" are also family terms in New Testament

13. B. Nicholas, *An Introduction to Roman Law* (Oxford: Clarendon, 1962), 66. See also Lassen, "Roman Family," 104–5; S. Dixon, *The Roman Family* (Baltimore: Johns Hopkins University Press, 1992), 1–11.

times.[14] One now can see why so many scholars love individual word studies. What seemed like an embarrassingly meager amount of data for study threatens to become overwhelming in its bulk because these kinds of kinship terms are found in abundance in the Epistles, and in many instances with literal and, more importantly, figurative familial implications. There could be other terms as well. There are a number of incidental references in the Epistles that allude to various family situations. These include the household codes in Eph. 5:22–6:9; Col. 3:18–4:1; and 1 Pet. 2:18–3:7, which refer to proper behavior.[15] There are also references to specific forms of behavior, such as the marriage of Christians to nonbelievers (1 Cor. 7:12–16; 1 Pet. 3:1–2), divorce (1 Cor. 7:10–16), problems with sexual passions (1 Cor. 7; 1 Pet. 1:14–16), and husband-and-wife relations and behavior (1 Cor. 11:1–16; 1 Thess. 4:6–7; Eph. 5:23; Col. 3:18; 1 Tim. 2:9–12; Titus 2:4–5; 1 Pet. 3:1–5).[16] These are all very interesting and certainly give insights into familial relations in specific instances during the time of the New Testament—problems that Paul and the other writers had to face.

There is a much larger familial framework in place in the New Testament that is worth discussing, however. In fact, it is arguable that, despite a number of literal uses of this "family"

14. Moxnes ("What Is Family?" 21) writes: "The terminology that we do find . . . is primarily used of the large households of prosperous people, who had slaves, servants and other dependants. This terminology indicates that the Roman family must be understood in the context of a slave society, a situation that affected paternalism, the raising of children and sexual relations. . . . From many sources we learn that slaves, as a matter of fact, were part of such households (e.g., 1 Cor 7:21–24; Philemon; Eph 6:5–9; Col 2:2–4:1; 1 Peter 2:18–25)." See also C. Osiek and D. L. Balch, *Families in the New Testament World: Households and House Churches* (Louisville: Westminster John Knox, 1997), 174–92.

15. On the household codes, see D. L. Balch, *Let Wives Be Submissive: The Domestic Code in I Peter*, SBLMS 26 (Atlanta: Scholars Press, 1981); idem, "Household Codes," in *Greco-Roman Literature and the New Testament*, ed. D. E. Aune, SBLSBS 21 (Atlanta: Scholars Press, 1988), 25–50; G. E. Cannon, *The Use of Traditional Materials in Colossians* (Macon, Ga.: Mercer University Press, 1983), 95–131.

16. All of these examples are from Moxnes, "What Is Family?" 25, 30–33. See also J. M. G. Barclay, "The Family as the Bearer of Religion in Judaism and Early Christianity," in *Constructing Early Christian Families*, ed. Moxnes, 66–80, esp. 72–78.

language, figurative use of "family" language permeates the epistolary material of the New Testament to the point of constituting a basic and constituent framework for analyzing fundamental relations in the early church. I do not have the space here to treat every example, but I wish to offer a brief survey of some of the usages of these terms to illustrate what I mean. I think that once I have selected a few examples, when you turn to the epistolary material, you too will see the pervasive presence of the notion of family.[17] Once I have treated a number of these instances briefly, I wish to discuss two particular examples because I think that they have theological significance that perhaps has been overlooked.

Here I wish to concentrate first on the language of "father" and "brother" as well as on several related terms used in the Epistles. There are numerous instances in these writings of the authors addressing members of their audience or referring to them as "brothers." For example, Paul asks why the Romans pass judgment on their brother (Rom. 14:10), and says not to place an obstacle before a brother (14:13), or destroy him (14:15), or cause him to stumble (14:21). The plural "brothers" is used in 1 Tim. 5:1. In fact, Paul singles out particular individuals to call them "brother," such as Sosthenes (1 Cor. 1:1), Apollos (1 Cor. 16:12), Titus (2 Cor. 2:13), Epaphroditus (Phil. 2:25), Tychicus (Col. 4:7), and Timothy (2 Cor. 1:1; 1 Thess. 3:2; Philem. 1). He clarifies what he means in 1 Cor. 5:11, when he speaks of anyone who bears the name of "brother," referring to members of the Christian community.[18] "Brother," therefore, seems to be the most widely used familial term in the Epistles, and it refers to other members of the Christian community. It is not only Paul who uses this language, however. The Books of Hebrews (8:11; 13:23), James (1:9; 2:15; 4:11), 1 and 2 Peter (1 Pet. 5:12; 2 Pet. 3:15, referring to "our brother Paul"), and 1 John (2:9, 10, 11; 3:10, 15, 17; 4:20, 21; 5:16) do the same.[19] The highest concentration of usage probably is in Philemon,

17. See Hellerman, *Ancient Church as Family*, 92–126, on Paul.
18. On the concept of brotherhood in Paul, see R. Aasgaard, "Brotherhood in Plutarch and Paul: Its Role and Character," in *Constructing Early Christian Families*, ed. Moxnes, 166–82, esp. 174–78.
19. For the sake of this essay, I classify all of these as epistles. For discussion, see McDonald and Porter, *Early Christianity*, 517–51, passim.

where Paul uses "brother" language four times as well as other familial language, as I note below. The first time "brother" is used with reference to Timothy (v. 1), the second time it is used of Philemon (v. 7), the third time of Onesimus (v. 16), and the fourth and final time again of Philemon in Paul's statement that he wants some benefit from the Lord (v. 20). The effect of common address is to place all of these people together on the same plane, including both Onesimus and Philemon.[20] Note also that there are a few instances of "sister" language being used similarly in the Epistles (Rom. 16:1, for Phoebe; Philem. 2, of Apphia; James 2:15; 1 Tim. 5:2 uses the plural).

"Child" language also is used in this metaphorical familial way, although not to the same extent. For example, Paul speaks of Timothy as his beloved and faithful child (1 Cor. 4:17; cf. 2 Tim. 1:2), Titus as his true child (Titus 1:4), and Onesimus as his child (Philem. 10). "Son" language is used surprisingly little in terms of any type of figurative familial usage, one of the few instances to note being Gal. 4:6, where Paul refers to the Galatians as "sons."

Terminology for "father" adds a further dimension to this set of figurative language. The epistles extensively refer to God as "father," usually as "our father" but also as "the father of Jesus Christ" (e.g., Rom. 1:7; 15:6; 1 Cor. 1:3; 8:6; 15:24; 2 Cor. 1:2, 3; 11:31; Gal. 1:1, 3, 4; 4:6; Eph. 1:2, 3; 2:18; 3:14; 4:6; 5:20; 6:23; Phil. 1:2; 2:11; 4:20; Col. 1:2, 3, 12; 3:17; 1 Thess. 1:1, 3; 3:11, 13; 2 Thess. 1:1, 2; 2:16; 1 Tim. 1:2; 2 Tim. 1:2; Titus 1:4; Philem. 3; 1 Pet. 1:2, 3, 17; 2 Pet. 1:17; 1 John 1:3; 2:1, 16, 22, 23, 24; 3:1; 4:14; 2 John 3, 4, 9; Jude 1).

This pattern of address has prompted a number of scholars, among them P. F. Esler, to note that members of the early Christian communities "did regard themselves as (fictive) brothers under a (fictive) father, their patron . . . and this may constitute a feature in Paul's social environment influencing his use of *adelphoi* [brothers] with respect to the Christ-followers in his congregations."[21] Esler neglects several features of the evidence, how-

20. See N. R. Petersen, *Rediscovering Paul: Philemon and the Sociology of Paul's Narrative World* (Philadelphia: Fortress, 1985).

21. P. F. Esler, "Family Imagery and Christian Identity in Gal 5:13 to 6:10," in *Constructing Early Christian Families*, ed. Moxnes, 121–49, esp. 136–37, quoting D. C. Duling, "The Matthean Brotherhood and Marginal Scribal Leadership," in *Modelling Early Christianity: Social-Scientific Studies of the New Testament in Its Context*, ed. P. F. Esler (London: Routledge, 1995), 159–82, here 163.

ever. One is that this pattern is found in much more than Paul's letters; it pervades the epistolary material, being found not only in Paul but also in the Petrines, Johannines, and Jude. There are, in fact, a number of references in the Petrine materials that are surprisingly similar to the Pauline references. This evidence indicates several further factors to consider. One is in regard to the origin and pervasiveness of this kind of language within the Christian community and outside of it. The issue depends to some extent on when one dates these various epistles, but it is at least arguable that the Pauline letters along with the Petrines and Johannines all attest to a widespread Christian practice at that time of addressing fellow Christians as "brothers." It appears that those who had a close relationship, in this case because of common belief in Jesus as the Christ, felt free to identify themselves with each other as "brother" and "sister." They used the language of family relations in order to capture the close affinity that they had with each other, an affinity that transcended the kinds of normal social boundaries and joined them together in a metaphorical sense within the closest set of personal associations known in the ancient world, the family. It is therefore logical also to think that what joins these brothers and sisters together is not only their common belief regarding Jesus but also their common allegiance to God, depicted as father.

There is no doubt a temptation, as reflected in Esler's comments, to see this as originating in the Pauline context, and perhaps being picked up by later Christian authors as well. However, this probably is not correct. The use of "brother" language to refer to those who are close associates is found in the Jesus material. In the Gospels, Jesus is depicted as referring to his followers, especially his disciples, with the term "brother" (e.g., Matt. 12:50; 28:10; Mark 3:35; John 20:17). It might be argued that this reflects later usage put into the mouth of Jesus, but the widespread use in the traditional Jesus material (multiple attestation) tends to indicate that this is authentic to what Jesus said.[22] The same is true for the use of father language. Jesus did

22. On this criterion for determining authentic Jesus material, see S. E. Porter, *The Criteria for Authenticity in Historical-Jesus Research: Previous Discussion and New Proposals*, JSNTSup 191 (Sheffield: Sheffield Academic Press, 2000), esp. 82–89.

not hesitate to address God as father, no doubt reflecting his own belief in his status in relation to God, but he also encouraged his followers to use similar language. For example, in the Lord's Prayer, the disciples are taught to pray, "Our Father . . ." (Matt. 6:9). The earliest followers of Jesus were encouraged to see him as a brother and to address God as father. This usage seems to be reflected in the Epistles as well.

It appears, however, that this language was not new or unique to Jesus. The language of "brother" and "father"—that is, family language shared by those who held common beliefs— seems to have been a common phenomenon of religious groups in the ancient Hellenistic and Greco-Roman worlds. The term "brother" is used of those who belong to a religious community in a number of documents from the Hellenistic world, such as a second-century-B.C.E. papyrus from hermits belonging to the Memphis Serapeum (P. Paris 20), or a papyrus from 117 B.C.E. referring to brothers who offer service among the dead, and a number of other inscriptions and papyri from this general period. This even includes reference by Josephus in *Jewish War* 2.122 to the Essenes calling each other "brother." So much is perhaps fairly commonly known. Less well known, but also worth noting, is that the language of "father" is similarly used. Not only do we have Old Testament and intertestamental usage of "father" for God, using the familial language, but also ancient Greek thought going back to before the time of Homer referred to Zeus as "father." It is fairly common to find among writers such as Pindar, Plato, and the later philosophers, such as Epictetus, Diogenes Laertius, and Maximus Tyrannus, and also Philo, references to God as "father," reflecting God's role as originator and ruler of the cosmos and father of humankind. Such usage is also found in Josephus (*Jewish Antiquities* 1.20; 4.262).[23] This evidence supports the notion that the ancient world was full of familial language used to describe, on a larger scale and by means of metaphorical reference, the kinds of intimate relations found within a family. This usage was carried over to the various religious groups of the first century, includ-

23. This evidence is from BDAG, s.v. ἀδελφός and πατήρ; see also A. Deissmann, *Bible Studies*, trans. A. J. Grieve (Edinburgh: Clark, 1901), 87–88, 142.

ing usage by Jesus and then by his followers, such as the authors of the Epistles.

Another shortcoming of Esler's analysis is that he overlooks
some of the particularities of usage. It is not simply that God is
seen as the patron. The relationship with God is seen to be more
complex. Some of these complexities I address in looking at
two particular usages.

"Slave" and "Master" Language

There are two types of usage that I examine here in more detail. The first is with reference to "slave" and "master" language.
"Master" language is limited in the Epistles, although it is
present, and this usage is worth noting. In Rom. 14:4, Paul says
that the "master" is able to make a fallen sinner stand; in 2 Pet.
2:1, Jesus is described as the "master" who "bought" certain
teachers who then will deny him; and in Jude 4, Jesus is called
"our only master and Lord." However, "slave" language is much
more prominent. Besides instances of literal usage (e.g., 1 Cor.
7:21, 22; Gal. 3:28; Col. 3:11; Philem. 16), there is also important
metaphorical usage. There are numerous references to someone
being God's servant (Rom. 13:4) and to Christ becoming a servant or slave (Rom. 15:8; Phil. 2:7), and especially to the author
or another Christian being a slave or servant of Jesus Christ
(Rom. 1:1; Phil. 1:1; Col. 1:7; 4:7, 12; 1 Thess. 3:2; 2 Tim. 2:24;
Titus 1:1; James 1:1; 2 Pet. 1:1; Jude 1).

As a result of these figurative usages of family language, it
does not come as a surprise that Michael Brown recently has
argued that the use by Paul of the phrase "slave of Christ Jesus"
in Rom. 1:1 is a technical term that Paul uses to refer to himself.
Paul places himself within the *familia Caesaris* as a member of
the royal slaves by this usage, a convention that directly addresses the situation of the audience in Rome.[24] I think that
Brown is essentially correct that Paul uses the phrase "slave of
Christ Jesus" as a self-identifier, but I do not see it as a technical
term by which he places himself within the *familia Caesaris*.
For one thing, it is not clearly established that the royal house-

24. M. J. Brown, "Paul's Use of Δοῦλος Χριστοῦ Ἰησοῦ in Romans 1:1," *JBL*
120, no. 4 (2001): 723–37.

hold played a major part in the Christian churches at Rome, and there is little that is particular to this usage here that indicates ties to the household. In fact, as Brown notes, there is plenty of anti-emperor language in the opening of Romans. Brown uses the reference to the family of Caesar to explain Rom. 13:1–7 with its apparent call to unqualified obedience to the state—an attempt to get at a difficult passage. I find his assumption regarding the meaning of the passage to be unwarranted and implausible, as I have argued elsewhere.[25] Brown notes, but does not fully appreciate, the fact that Paul uses similar terminology of himself in other letters as well, such as Gal. 1:10, where he refers to himself as a "slave of Christ"; or Phil. 1:1, where both Paul and Timothy are called "slaves of Christ Jesus"; or Titus 1:1, where Paul describes himself as a "slave of God and apostle of Jesus Christ" (an instance that Brown dismisses because it is not in the undisputed letters). In Col. 4:12, Paul calls Epaphroditus a "slave of Christ [Jesus]." I note also that 2 Pet. 1:1 and Jude 1 use a similar introduction, with Peter or Jude referring to himself as a "slave of Christ Jesus." Further, in James 1:1 the author identifies himself as a "slave of God and of the Lord Jesus Christ." What makes this pattern of usage important in familial terms is not the use of "slave" language as a technical term but the link of that particular person's name to Christ, that someone is a slave of Christ (or in Phil. 1:1, the link to two persons' names). What is also clear from this evidence is that a number of writers of the New Testament Epistles, including Paul, Peter, Jude, and James, saw themselves as slaves of Jesus Christ, with all that the notion of slavery indicated in the ancient world.[26]

This might strike some as an odd mix of metaphors—familial and slave—and perhaps a pushing of the metaphor of family too far, since it is Jesus who is seen as the slave owner in the metaphor of being the servant of Jesus. But perhaps not. As Nicholas has made clear, it is the father of the family who owned everything and who, in a way that we cannot even imag-

25. See S. E. Porter, "Romans 13:1–7 as Pauline Political Rhetoric," *FN* 3, no. 6 (1990): 115–39.
26. See K. R. Bradley, *Slaves and Masters in the Roman Empire: A Study in Social Control* (New York: Oxford University Press, 1987); T. Wiedemann, ed., *Greek and Roman Slavery* (London: Croom Helm, 1981).

ine today, exercised supreme authority as the only one with full human rights under Roman law, even the power of life and death. Thus, according to the law, a son could not own anything; whatever he did acquire was automatically owned by the *paterfamilias*. Due to the inconvenience of this situation, however, "it became customary for the *paterfamilias* to allow his son the free use of some property (his *peculium*), and in particular of such property as he acquired by his own exertions."[27] In one sense, there is no language more fitting than slave language in which the believer is linked to Christ, since it is by his exertions on the cross that the believer comes to be owned by him (see 1 Cor. 7:22–23). Thus, the language of slavery can be seen to fit within the familial metaphor as well, in the sense that those who are servants of Jesus Christ are the property of the son of the family, purchased by his actions even though ultimately possessed by God.

Galatians and Sonship

The last passage I would like to explore exemplifies some of the implications of the familial language in relation to God. As I have noted, there are a number of passages in which God is depicted simply as the "father" (e.g., Rom. 6:4; 1 Cor. 8:6; Gal. 1:3; Eph. 6:23), but there are also a number of passages in which he is depicted as "our father" or words to that effect (e.g., Rom 1:7; 1 Cor. 1:3; 2 Cor. 1:2; Phil. 1:2; cf. Gal. 1:4) and a number of passages in which God is depicted as the father of Jesus Christ (e.g., Rom. 15:6; 2 Cor. 1:3; 11:31; Eph. 1:3; Col. 1:3).

It is clear from elsewhere in Paul's writings that Paul was an incipient trinitarian. For example, in 2 Cor. 13:13 he speaks of the "grace of the Lord Jesus Christ, the love of God, and the communion of the Holy Spirit" (NRSV), using three parallel phrases. Each of these consists of a structure in which there is a head term depicting beneficence linked to a figure seen elsewhere in the Pauline writings as a divine figure, here arranged in a parallelism that is hard to refute as being trinitarian. More poignantly, Rom. 1:1–4 defines a complex relationship in which God promises through his prophets regard-

27. Nicholas, *Roman Law*, 68.

ing the gospel, which is about God's son, who was declared
Son of God by the Spirit of holiness. In this depiction, we have
within the familial sphere a father God and his son, Jesus
Christ (note also the language of "firstborn" in Rom. 8:29; Col.
1:15, 18). There may be an economic trinity (if such wording
is fair to use), but it is descriptive of differentiated functions
within a complex relation of divine beings. This framework is
important, however, since it makes sense not only of the traditional sonship passages noted above but also of a number of
passages in which familial language is used of one of the
members of this trinity but not of the other, even though the
two are described similarly (e.g., Rom. 1:7; 1 Cor. 1:3; 2 Cor.
1:2; Gal. 1:3; Eph. 1:2; 6:23; Phil. 1:2; 1 Thess. 1:1; 2 Thess. 1:2;
1 Tim. 1:2; Philem. 3), as in "God our Father and the Lord
Jesus Christ." I note that usage of these phrases often appears
near the beginning of a Pauline letter. Though they do not explicitly state it, within the context that I have described, these
passages seem to me to be implicit, secondary statements affirming the deity of Jesus Christ by Paul or at least expressing
his view that Jesus Christ is of the same status as God the Father. Of course, there are plenty of other passages in which
Paul works this notion out more systematically (e.g., Phil. 2:6–
11; Col. 1:15–20), but I believe that it is for Paul a common-
place rooted to some extent in his metaphorical familial language of relationship.

There are two further sets of references that potentially
cloud the situation, however. There are a number of passages,
already noted, in which Jesus addresses his followers as brothers (and sisters), and in which God is depicted as the father of
believers. How do we understand this complex relationship, in
light of the preceding discussion, especially one that includes
slavery? One might wish to elevate human beings to the level of
the divine, having equal status with God and the divine Son
(something along the lines of God = Jesus, and Jesus = humans,
so God and Jesus = humans). I do not think that this is the correct understanding. Others are inclined to leave them as tensions between a hierarchical and egalitarian framework within
Paul's thought, in which the hierarchical one was giving way to
the egalitarian one. There is some merit to this because it is entirely possible that there are competing metaphors at work in

the New Testament.[28] However, I think that what is being said here is that our rightful position, as Paul and other epistolary writers so aptly describe it, is that we are entitled to the status of slaves of God and of Jesus Christ. That is our rightful status within God's family. It is as possessions of the *paterfamilias* that we exist within God's family, but we have been liberated from this position and elevated to the position of sons and daughters of God. Paul explicates this idea well in Galatians. There is much that could be said about what Paul conveys in Galatians regarding the law, Judaism, and especially the family. Here I wish to concentrate on the last of these to explicate how the familial language has bearing on understanding our position in God's family.

In Gal. 3, Paul is explicating his understanding of the law in relation not only to the Galatians but also to the history of salvation. He says in 3:23 that before faith, we were kept in custody under the law, which he equates in 3:24 with a "tutor" (παιδαγωγός, *paidagōgos*).[29] The παιδαγωγός was a slave within the household who had responsibility for keeping an eye on the child of the family.[30] Paul says that now that faith has come, we are not under the παιδαγωγός any more (3:25), but that we are "sons of God" through faith in Christ Jesus (3:26). In Gal. 4:1, Paul aptly states that "as long as the heir is a child, he does not differ at all from a slave, although he is owner of everything," which is indeed an accurate reflection of Roman law. Even though the child would inherit the estate, before the death of the father he had the same status as a slave—that is, he was owned by the *paterfamilias*. As Nicholas says, "In early law there was evidently little difference between son and slave, both being regarded as the property of the *paterfamilias* to be disposed of as he wished."[31] However, Paul says, in the fullness of

28. K. O. Sandnes, "Equality within Patriarchal Structures: Some New Testament Perspectives on the Christian Fellowship as a Brother- or Sisterhood and a Family," in *Constructing Early Christian Families*, ed. Moxnes, 150–65.

29. See B. Rawson, "Adult-Child Relationships in Roman Society," in *Marriage, Divorce, and Children in Ancient Rome*, ed. B. Rawson (Oxford: Clarendon, 1991), 7–30.

30. See F. Mussner, *Der Galaterbrief*, HTKNT 9 (Freiburg: Herder, 1977), 256–58.

31. Nicholas, *Roman Law*, 66.

time God sent his Son to redeem us so that "we might receive the adoption as sons" (4:5):[32] "Therefore you are no longer a slave, but a son; and if a son, then an heir through God" (4:7). This too reflects Roman procedure, in which "the formalities for the emancipation and adoption of sons were in essentials the same as those used for the conveyance of property."[33] We who were slaves have been consciously bought and elevated to become adopted sons and daughters of God. Paul exhorts his readers in Galatia, "It was for freedom that Christ set us free; therefore keep standing firm and do not be subject again to a yoke of slavery" (5:1). Not only is it the work of Christ that purchases our status as sons of God, but also it is the continued guidance of the Spirit (5:16–18). It is this elevation of status from slave to adopted son of God that allows us to be called brothers and sisters and to call each other brother and sister within the "household of faith" (6:10).

Conclusion

The familial language in the Epistles of the New Testament is highly complex. Using literal categories, the authors have spiritually conceptualized them to create a complex set of metaphors regarding the family of God. This family consists of its human members, who, rather than use the merited title of slave, as the redeemed of Christ can call each other brother and sister. It also consists of relationships with God as father and with his son Jesus Christ as our fellow brother because of our adoptive sonship. This familial relation also indicates the divinity of Christ. The result is that we are a part of the family of faith.

I do not usually end essays in this way, but in this instance, I cannot help but note that one song by the Gaithers captures ex-

32. For a treatment of adoption language, but one that does not do full justice to the Greco-Roman background of the term's use in the New Testament, see J. M. Scott, *Adoption as Sons of God: An Exegetical Investigation into the Background of Huiothesia in the Pauline Corpus*, WUNT 2.48 (Tübingen: Mohr Siebeck, 1992).

33. Nicholas, *Roman Law*, 66.

ceedingly well what the Epistles say regarding our familial relationship with God. The song declares,

> I'm so glad I'm a part of the family of God—
> I've been washed in the fountain [here, I wish they had said
>   something like "filled by the Spirit"], cleansed by His blood!
> Joint heirs with Jesus as we travel this sod—
> For I'm part of the family, the family of God.[34]

34. Gloria and William J. Gaither, "The Family of God," © copyright 1970.

Index of Scripture and Other Ancient Writings

Genesis

1 25, 26
1–2 29
1:26–28 34
1:28 25, 127, 139, 146 n. 64
2 25, 26, 27, 28, 30
2:18 17
2:23 25, 68
2:24 18, 27, 67, 131
2:25 27
3 25, 27, 28
3:7–8 27
4 28
5:1–3 34
6 28
6:5 28
6:11 28
6:13 28
8:21 28
9:22 28
12:2 25
12:7 64
12:10–20 28
13:2–18 30
13:14–17 29
13:16 25
16 29
19:8 25, 72
19:30–38 28
20:1–18 28
21:25–32 30
22:2 25, 72
22:16–18 29
24 65
24:28 61
24:47 65
24:50 66
24:50–51 23
25–35 29
26:6–11 28
26:26–33 30
29–30 26
29:14 26
29:22–29 24
29:31 28
29:32 26
29:33 26
29:34 26
30:1 25
30:18 26
30:20 26
30:24 27
31 22
33:4 30
34:30 30
35:22 28
37–50 29
42:1–2 22
43:1–2 22
44:27 28
45:3 30
49 30
49:4 28

Exodus

19–24 50
20 50
20:4–6 50
20:12 37 n. 5, 65, 72
20:14 129
20:17 129
21:1–11 111
21:2–6 38
21:15 37 n. 5, 40, 72
21:17 37, 40, 72
22:22 71
22:23–24 71
23:6–11 38

Leviticus

18 38
20 38
20:9 37 n. 5
25 31, 38
25:10 64
25:25 66
25:25–28 37
25:25–55 111

Numbers

27:8–9 38
27:9–11 38
30 22
36:7–9 37

Deuteronomy

1–4 46
1:5 44 n. 22
1:35 43
1:38–39 43
1:39 43
4:1 43
4:1–9 43
4:3 49 n. 38
4:5 43
4:9 43
4:9–10 50
4:10 43
4:14 43
4:15–20 43
4:15–40 49 n. 38
4:25 43
4:25–28 43
4:29–31 43
4:37 48
4:39 43
4:39–40 43
4:44–30:20 43 n. 18
5 50
5–11 45, 46
5:1 43, 44
5:2–3 43
5:3 44
5:7–10 49 n. 38
5:8–10 50
5:16 37 n. 5
5:24 44
5:29 43
5:31 43
5:32–33 43
6:1 43
6:1–3 43, 50
6:2–3 43

6:4 48, 51
6:4–5 47, 48, 52
6:4–7 50
6:4–9 41, 46, 47, 50, 55, 57
6:4–25 47
6:5 48, 49
6:5–7 49
6:6 44, 47, 51
6:6–9 48
6:7 43, 49, 51, 65
6:7–9 51
6:7–10 43
6:9 51
6:10–25 49
6:12 44
6:13–14 49
6:20–25 43, 50, 51
7:3–4 68
7:4–5 49 n. 38
7:7–8 48
7:9 43
7:16 49 n. 38
7:25 49 n. 38
8:1 43
8:16 43
8:19 44, 49 n. 38
9:5 43
9:12 49 n. 38
9:16 49 n. 38
9:26–29 64
10:11 43
10:15 43, 48
10:18 71
10:19 71
10:20–21 49 n. 38
11:2 43
11:7 43
11:16 49 n. 38
11:18–20 43, 46
11:18–32 50
11:19 43, 65
11:21 43
11:28 49 n. 38
12–26 43 n. 18, 45, 46
14:28–29 112

15:1–8 111
15:1–18 38
16:9–14 112
21:18–21 40, 72, 118
22:13–24 38
22:29 23 n. 6
24:1–4 38, 121, 131
24:6 38
24:10–15 38
24:17–22 38
24:19 71
24:19–21 112
25:5–6 66
25:5–10 38, 111
26:12 112
27–30 45, 46
27:8 44 n. 22
27:15 49 n. 38
27:16 37 n. 5, 40, 72
28:14 49 n. 38
29:10 43
29:14–15 43, 44
29:17–18 49 n. 38
29:22 43
29:26 49 n. 38
29:29 43, 44
29:29–30:10 50
30 50
31 46
31–34 46
31:13 43
32 46
33 46
34 47

Joshua
2:12 59, 60
2:18 60
4:6 65
4:7 65
4:21 65
4:23 65
6:23 60
6:25 60
7 62
7:1 61, 62

7:14–18 35
7:16 61
7:16–18 61, 105
7:18 61
7:21 62
22:20 62
24 50
24:14 60
24:15 50, 60

Judges
3:9 73
3:15 73
3:31 73
8:31 62
9:1 61, 62
11:2 63
11:30–31 72
11:39 72
13:2 70
13:24 69
14–16 50
14:2 23
14:3 65
14:12 24
17–18 35
17:6 72
18:19 105
19:24 72
21:25 72

Ruth
1:3–5 70
1:8 62
1:12–13 66
1:16 68
2:2–7 72
4:1–2 65
4:5 67
4:6 67
4:9–22 67
4:15 70 n. 25

1 Samuel
1 70
1:3 63
1:5 68
1:6–7 68
1:8 68

1:10–11 139
2:5 70
2:6 72
2:12 50
2:17 50, 73
2:22 73
2:22–25 50
2:28 63
2:29 73
2:29–36 50
2:34 73
3:13 73
3:13–14 50
4:11 73
4:17 73
4:17–22 50
4:21 69
8 63
8:1 63
8:1–2 73
8:1–5 50
8:3 73
8:5–7 63
9:2 74
9:5 74
9:16 64
9:20 61
10:1 64
10:2 74
10:20–21 61
12:3–5 73
13:2 74
13:13–14 63
14:6 74
16:11 75
16:17–20 65
16:18 63
17:12 66 n. 17
17:13 63
17:28 75
19:1 74
19:6 74
20:2 74
20:6 61, 66
20:12 74
20:29 66, 75
20:31 63
20:34 74
22:1 75

22:3 75
22:8 74
22:20 63
25:1 77
26:19 64
28:3 77

2 Samuel

3:2–3 75
3:4 77
12–1 Kings 1
12:24 69
12:24–25 69
13:21 75
13:22 75
13:34 62, 75
13:37 75, 76
14 75
14:24 76
14:28 76
14:33 76
15:30 76
18:12 76
18:18 69
18:33 77
19:2 77
19:37 77
21:11–14 77

1 Kings

1:5 77
1:6 77
1:17 77
1:20 77
2:10 77
3:1 68
11 50
11:1–3 68
11:2 68
11:4 68
11:5 68
11:7 68
16:31 69
17:17 70
21 64, 114
21:3 64

2 Kings

4:14 69

4:16 70
16:3 72
17:17 72
21:6 50, 72
22–23 50

Ezra

9 68
9:2 126 n. 7
10 68

Nehemiah

10:30 68
13:23–37 68

Job

1:2 70 n. 25
42:13 70 n. 25

Psalms

14:1 87
29:10 63
44:1 37 n. 5
68:6 17
78:4–8 37 n. 5
78:71 64
94:5 64
127 96 n. 13
127:3 69, 72
128:3 69

Proverbs

1–9 81, 84, 94
1:2–3 87
1:2–7 86
1:4 87
1:5 87
1:7 87
1:8 73, 84
1:8–9 37 n. 5
1:22 87
2:16 92
2:16–22 91
3:13–18 91
4:3–4 84
4:4–9 91
5 91
5:15–20 92

6:16–19 83
6:20 73, 84
6:20–22 37 n. 5
6:20–35 91
6:24–29 91
7 91, 92
7:5 92
7:10 92
9 94
9:1–6 94
9:13–18 95
10:1 37 n. 5,
  85 n. 9
11:21 90
11:22 94
11:29 83
12:4 93
13:1 85 n. 9
13:24 37 n. 5
14:1 84
15:5 37 n. 5,
  85 n. 9
15:20 37 n. 5,
  85 n. 9
15:32 37 n. 5
15:33 37 n. 5
17:6 90
17:21 85 n. 9
17:25 85 n. 9
18:22 93
19:26 85 n. 9
20:7 90
20:20 85
21:9 93
21:19 93
22:6 88
22:14 92
22:15 87, 90
23:13–14 88
24:3 95
25:11 82
25:20 82
25:24 93
26:4–5 83
26:7 82
26:9 82
27:8 83
27:15–16 93
28:7 85 n. 9

28:24 85 n. 9
29:3 85 n. 9
29:15 88
30:11–14 85
30:17 37 n. 5,
  85
30:19 99
31 23, 93
31:1 84
31:1–31 93
31:11–31 39
31:26 37 n. 5
31:30 94

Ecclesiastes

1:1–11 98
4:9–12 97
7:25–29 97
12:8–14 98
12:12 98
12:13–14 98

Song of Songs

3:4 61
8:2 61
8:6–7 99

Isaiah

1:3 118
1:10–2:5 114
1:17 71, 113
1:23 113
3:16–4:1 114
5:8 114
8:19–20 110
10:1–2 113
19:25 64
41:14 121
43:14 121
46:3–4 119
47:8–9 70
49:13–15 119
50:1–3 121
52:1–2 119
54:1–10 121
54:5 121
57 110
57:3–13 110
57:6–7 110

57:9 110
62:11 119
63:16 117, 121
64:7 MT 117
64:8 117
65:2–5 110
66:12–14 119

Jeremiah

2–4 120
3:1–5 121
3:4 121
3:5 118
3:14 121
3:19 118, 121
4:31 119
5:26–29 113
7:1–15 114
7:16–19 109
7:30–32 110
14:17–18 119
15:9 70 n. 25
16:5–9 110 n. 22
19:4–6 110
19:12–13 109
22:3 113
31:9 119
32:6–15 111
32:29 109
32:35 110
34:8–22 113
34:12–16 121
44:15–25 109
50:34 121

Ezekiel

16 101, 102, 120,
  121
16:1–19 118
16:15–18 102
16:21 110
16:25–37 102
16:38–42 102
16:59–63 102
20:31 110
23 101, 102, 120
23:1–22 102
23:24–35 102

23:39 110
23:40–49 102

Hosea

1–3 101, 120
2:2–13 101
2:4–15 MT 101
2:14–23 101
2:16–25 MT 101
4 108 n. 15
4:13–14 108
6:4–6 114
11:1–7 118
11:8 119

Joel

2:17 64

Amos

2:6 113
2:7 108 n. 16
2:7–8 108
2:8 108 n. 16
3:1–2 61 n. 9
4:1 114
4:4–5 114
5:4–6 114
5:11–24 114
6:4–6 110 n. 22,
  114
7:14 63 n. 12
8:6 113

Micah

2:1–2 114
4:10 119
6:6–8 114

Zephaniah

1:5 109
3:14 119

Zechariah

7:10 113
9:9 119

Malachi

2:10 117 n. 33

2:10–3:15 114
2:11–12 109
2:13–14 109
3:5 113
4:6 37 n. 5

Sirach

3:1–16 39

Matthew

2:19–23 142
5:27–28 126
5:27–30 126
5:31 131 n. 24
5:31–32 126, 130
6:9 133, 159
8:14 138
8:19–20 137
8:21–22 138
10:9–10 138
10:34–37 136
12:50 158
17:25–27 133
18:1–5 126, 127,
  127 n. 10
19:1–9 126, 130,
  131
19:3 131 n. 25
19:3–12
  131 n. 25
19:12 139
19:13–15 126,
  127
22:24 66
23:8–10 133
28:10 158

Mark

1:16–18 137
1:19–20 137
3:20–21 144
3:31–35 133,
  136, 144,
  144 n. 62
3:35 136 n. 40,
  158
6:1–6 143
6:8–9 138
6:17 144 n. 61

7:9–13 126, 129
9:33–37 126,
  127, 127 n. 10
10:1–12 126, 130
10:13–16
  127 n. 10
10:14 127 n. 9
10:28–30 138
10:29–30 133
12:12 144 n. 61
12:19 66
13:9–13 136,
  136 n. 39
13:13 136 n. 39
13:17–19 139
14:1 144 n. 61
14:44 144 n. 61
14:46 144 n. 61
14:49 144 n. 61
14:51 144 n. 61

Luke

1:24 69
1:25 139
1:26–27 142–43
1:56 142 n. 57
2:4 149
2:5 142 n. 57
2:44 143
2:49 142
2:51 145
7:11–15 70
8:1–3 138
8:19–21 133
9:3 138
9:46–48 126, 127
9:59–60 138
9:61–62 138
10:4 138
11:11–13 133
11:27 144
11:27–28 136
14:12–14 137
14:26 136
15:11–32 133,
  137
16:18 126, 130
18:15–17 126,
  127
23:28–30 139

John

3:16 133
7:1–9 143
7:53–8:11 130,
    130 n. 18
8:41 143
10:25–33 133
19:25 144
19:26–27 144
20:17 158

Acts

1:14 140, 145
3:25 149
12:17 145
15:14 145
19:14 70 n. 25
21:18 145

Romans

1:1 160
1:1–4 162
1:7 157, 162, 163
6:4 162
8:29 163
13:1–7 161
13:4 160
14:4 160
14:10 156
14:13 156
14:15 156
14:21 156
15:4 19, 30
15:6 157, 162
15:8 160
16:1 157
16:5 152

1 Corinthians

1:1 156
1:3 157, 162, 163
1:16 152
4:17 157
5:11 156
7 155
7:8–38 139
7:10–16 155
7:12–16 155

7:21 160
7:21–24
    155 n. 14
7:22 160
7:22–23 162
8:6 157, 162
11:1–16 155
11:22 153
11:34 152
13:11 127 n. 10
14:20 127 n. 10
14:35 152
15:24 157
16:12 156
16:15 153
16:19 152

2 Corinthians

1:1 156
1:2 157, 162, 163
1:3 157, 162
2:13 156
5:1 153
11:31 157, 162
13:13 162

Galatians

1:1 157
1:3 157, 162, 163
1:4 157, 162
1:10 161
3 164
3:23 164
3:24 164
3:25 164
3:26 164
3:28 160
4:1 164
4:5 165
4:6 157
4:7 165
5:1 165
5:16–18 165
6:10 153, 165

Ephesians

1:2 157, 163
1:3 157, 162
2:18 157

2:19 153
3:14 157
3:14–15 149
3:15 149
4:6 157
5 18
5:20 157
5:22–6:9 155
5:23 155
6:1 73
6:5–9 155 n. 14
6:23 157, 162, 163

Philippians

1:1 160, 161
1:2 157, 162, 163
2:6–11 163
2:7 160
2:11 157
2:25 156
4:20 157
4:22 153

Colossians

1:2 157
1:3 157, 162
1:7 160
1:12 157
1:15 163
1:15–20 163
1:18 163
2:2–4:1 155 n. 14
3:11 160
3:17 157
3:18 155
3:18–4:1 155
4:7 156, 160
4:12 160, 161
4:15 152

1 Thessalonians

1:1 157, 163
1:3 157
3:2 156, 160
3:11 157
3:13 157
4:6–7 155

2 Thessalonians

1:1 157
1:2 157, 163
2:16 157

1 Timothy

1:2 157, 163
2:9–12 155
3:4 152
3:5 152
3:12 152
5:1 156
5:2 157
5:3 72
5:4 152
5:5 72
5:8 153
5:13 153
5:16 72

2 Timothy

1:2 157
1:16 152
2:20 153
2:24 160
3:6 153
4:19 152

Titus

1:1 160, 161
1:4 157
1:11 152
2:4–5 155

Philemon

1 156, 157
2 152, 157
3 157, 163
7 157
10 157
16 157, 160
20 157

Hebrews

3:2 152
3:3 152

3:4 152
3:5 152
3:6 152
5:13 127 n. 10
8:8 152
8:10 152
8:11 156
10:21 152
11:7 152
13:23 156

James

1:1 160, 161
1:6 127 n. 10
1:9 156
1:23 152
2:15 156, 157
3:6 152
4:11 156

1 Peter

1:2 157
1:3 157
1:14–16 155
1:17 157
2:2 127 n. 10
2:5 152

2:18–25
  155 n. 14
2:18–3:7 155
3:1–2 155
3:1–5 155
4:17 152
5:12 156

2 Peter

1:1 160, 161
1:17 157
2:1 160
3:15 156

1 John

1:3 157
2:1 157
2:9 156
2:10 156
2:11 156
2:16 157
2:22 157
2:23 157
2:24 157
3:1 157
3:10 156
3:15 156

3:17 156
4:14 157
4:19 48
4:20 156
4:21 156
5:16 156

2 John

3 157
4 157
9 157
10 153

Jude

1 157, 160, 161
4 160

Josephus

*Jewish
  Antiquities*

  1.20 159
  4.262 159

Jewish War

  2.122 159

Papyri

P. Paris

  20 159

Ugaritic Texts

KTU

  1.15.II.23 70
    n. 25
  1.16.VI.33–
    34 71
  1.16.VI.49–
    50 71
  1.17.I.26 78
  1.17.V.7–8 71
  1.23.8–9 70
  1.23.56–
    57 69

UT

  52.8–9 70
  52.56–57 69
  128.II.23 70
    n. 25

Index of Modern Authors

Aasgaard, R. 156 n. 18
Abma, R. 117 n. 30, 117 n. 32, 118 n. 34
Achtemeier, Elizabeth 43 n. 17, 46 n. 26
Ackerman, Susan 109 n. 18, 110 n. 21, 110 n. 22
Allender, D. 93 n. 12
Alonso Schökel, Luis 104 n. 9
Alvez, Rubén 53 n. 40

Babb, O. J. 36, 41 n. 10
Balch, D. L. 125 n. 3, 131 n. 25, 132 n. 26, 132 n. 29, 133 n. 32, 134 n. 33, 136 n. 39, 137, 138, 155 n. 14, 155 n. 15
Barclay, J. M. G. 134, 135 n. 34, 155 n. 16
Barclay, William 37 n. 5
Barr, James 151
Bartholomew, C. G. 20 n. 2
Barton, S. C. 134 n. 33, 136 n. 40, 139 n. 47, 141 n. 52, 143 n. 60, 144 n. 62
Bellis, Alice Ogden 101 n. 1
Benjamin, Don C. 102 n. 3, 106 n. 11
Best, E. 149 n. 1, 150 n. 3
Bird, Phyllis A. 60 n. 3, 76 n. 30, 108 n. 14, 109 n. 19
Bloch-Smith, Elizabeth 110 n. 22
Block, Daniel I. 103 n. 5
Blomberg, C. 127 n. 8, 127 n. 9
Bradley, K. R. 161 n. 26
Brenner, Athalaya 101 n. 2

Brichto, H. C. 62, 64 n. 13
Briend, Jacques 43, 44 n. 19
Bromiley, G. W. 151 n. 5
Brown, Michael J. 160, 161
Brueggeman, Walter 116 n. 29
Burrows, M. 24 n. 7

Campbell, Edward F. 106 n. 12
Cannon, G. E. 155 n. 15
Carney, T. F. 128 n. 11
Carroll R., M. Daniel 8 n. 1, 9, 112 n. 25, 114 n. 28
Carson, D. A. 143
Childs, Brevard S. 42 n. 14, 44 n. 22, 46 n. 25, 46 n. 27, 98
Clapp, R. 136
Clines, David J. A. 29, 114 n. 27
Cross, Frank M. 111 n. 23, 117 n. 32

Darr, Katheryn Pfisterer 101 n. 2
Dearman, John Andrew 112 n. 25
Deissmann, A. 159 n. 23
Dempsey, Carol J. 101 n. 1
deSilva, D. A. 141 n. 52
Dillard, R. B. 81 n. 4
Dixon, S. 154 n. 13
Driver, G. R. 23 n. 6
Duling, D. C. 157 n. 21

Eagleson, J. 53 n. 39
Ellis, I. 135 n. 37
Emmerson, Grace I. 102 n. 3
Esler, P. F. 157, 158
Exum, J. Cheryl 101 n. 2

173

Falk, Ze'ev W. 38 n. 7
Fontaine, C. 82 n. 6
Fox, Michael V. 84 n. 7, 96 n. 17
Fraser, E. R. 140 n. 49
Friedrich, G. 151

Gadamer, Hans-Georg 104 n. 9
Gaither, Gloria 166 n. 34
Gaither, William J. 166 n. 34
Galambush, Julie 101 n. 2, 117 n. 29, 118 n. 34
Gangel, K. O. 125 n. 1, 125 n. 5, 133 n. 30
García López, Félix 47 n. 32, 49 n. 37
Garrett, Duane A. 103 n. 5
Gaventa, B. R. 141 n. 51, 141 n. 54, 144 n. 63
Goleman, D. 80 n. 1
Gordon, C. H. 65 n. 16
Gordon, Robert P. 63 n. 11
Gottwald, Norman K. 105 n. 10
Grabbe, Lester L. 112 n. 25
Grieve, A. J. 159 n. 23
Guang T., Enrique 33 n. 1
Guijarro, S. 153 n. 10
Gunn, David 74 n. 29

Haak, Robert D. 112 n. 25
Hadley, Judith M. 119 n. 37
Hagedorn, Anselm C. 41 n. 9
Hagner, D. A. 127 n. 8
Hamilton, V. 86 n. 10
Harvey, A. E. 131 n. 24
Hasel, Gerhard 42 n. 13
Healey, J. F. 78 n. 31
Hellerman, J. H. 149 n. 2, 156 n. 17
Henry, Matthew 26
Hess, Richard S. 8 n. 1, 61 n. 7
Hildebrandt, T. 89 n. 11
Holladay, John S., Jr. 106 n. 12, 107 n. 13
Holladay, William L. 43 n. 16
Hubbard, David Allen 103 n. 5
Hubbard, Robert L., Jr. 66 n. 18, 68 n. 21
Hugenberger, Gordon P. 24 n. 7, 109 n. 17

Janzen, Waldemar 112 n. 24
Jaramillo Rivas, Pedro 120 n. 38
John Paul II 33 n. 1

Keel, Othmar 107 n. 13, 109 n. 20
Keener, C. 127 n. 8, 127 n. 9, 128 n. 13, 129, 130 n. 17, 130 n. 19, 130 n. 20, 131 n. 22, 141 n. 50, 141 n. 53, 142 n. 56, 143 n. 58
King, Philip J. 102 n. 3, 105 n. 10, 106 n. 12, 107 n. 13, 110 n. 22
Kirschenblatt-Gimblett, B. 82 n. 6
Kittel, G. 151
Kohl, M. 37 n. 5

Lacey, W. K. 142 n. 55
Lambdin, Thomas O. 48 n. 33
Landy, Francis 98
Lane, W. L. 129 n. 15
Lassen, E. M. 153 n. 12, 154 n. 13
Leichter, Hope J. 54 n. 41
Lewis, N. 128 n. 13
Lewis, Theodore J. 78 n. 32, 110 n. 22
Lincoln, A. 150 n. 3
Longman III, Tremper 9, 81 n. 4, 81 n. 5, 93 n. 12, 96 n. 16, 99 n. 21, 99 n. 23
Louw, J. P. 151, 152
Luis Sicre, José 53 n. 39

MacDonald, M. Y. 150 n. 3
Matthews, Victor H. 102 n. 3, 106 n. 11
Mayes, A. D. H. 45 n. 23
Mazar, Amihai 22 n. 4
McBride, Dean 45 n. 23, 47
McConville, J. G. 45 n. 23
McDonald, L. M. 150 n. 4, 156 n. 19
McKeating, Henry 118 n. 35
Meyers, Carol 22 n. 4, 23 n. 5, 34, 35, 38, 39, 102, 106 n. 11, 112 n. 25
Míguez Bonino, José 53 n. 40
Miles, J. C. 23 n. 6
Miller, Patrick D. 107 n. 13, 109 n. 19
Moberly, R. W. L. 103 n. 5
Moran, W. L. 49 n. 36
Moritz, T. 20 n. 2
Moxnes, H. 153 n. 11, 155 n. 14, 155 n. 16
Munro, Jill M. 99
Murphy, Roland E. 98, 99 n. 20
Mussner, F. 164 n. 30
Myers, C. 144 n. 61

Newsom, C. A. 101 n. 1, 101 n. 2
Nicholas, B. 154, 161, 162 n. 27, 164, 165 n. 33
Nicholson, E. W. 45 n. 23, 47 n. 30
Nida, E. A. 151, 152
Nielsen, K. 67 n. 19
Noth, Martin 42 n. 12, 46 n. 26

Ortlund, Raymond C., Jr. 103 n. 5
Osiek, C. 125 n. 3, 131 n. 25, 132 n. 26, 132 n. 29, 133 n. 32, 134 n. 33, 136 n. 39, 137, 138, 155 n. 14

Pardee, D. 71 n. 27, 71 n. 28, 78 n. 31
Parker, Simon B. 60 n. 4
Perdue, Leo G. 106 n. 11, 111 n. 23, 117 n. 31
Petersen, N. R. 157 n. 20
Pitre, B. J. 139 n. 45
Porfirio Miranda, José 53 n. 39
Porter, S. E. 10, 150 n. 4, 152 n. 8, 156 n. 19, 158 n. 22, 161 n. 25
Pryor, J. W. 125 n. 4, 133 n. 31, 133 n. 32

Rad, Gerhard von 47 n. 29, 47 n. 30
Rawson, B. 164 n. 29
Renan, E. 125 n. 2
Rendsburg, G. A. 65 n. 16
Richard, Pablo 53 n. 39
Rimmon-Kenan, S. 25
Ringe, S. H. 101 n. 1, 101 n. 2
Rodd, Cyril S. 103
Rushdoony, R. J. 146 n. 64
Russell, J. C. 132 n. 28
Rylaarsdam, J. C. 41 n. 11

Sánchez, Edesio 9
Sandnes, K. O. 164 n. 28
Schloen, J. D. 60 n. 4
Schmidt, Brian B. 110 n. 22
Schüssler Fiorenza, E. 125 n. 3
Scott, J. M. 165 n. 32
Setel, T. Drorah 101 n. 2
Sherwood, Yvonne 101 n. 2
Sim, D. C. 125 n. 6, 138 n. 44

Smith, Mark S. 107 n. 13, 110 n. 21, 110 n. 22, 119 n. 37
Stager, Lawrence E. 34, 35 n. 2, 61 n. 6, 102 n. 3, 105 n. 10, 106 n. 11, 106 n. 12, 107 n. 13, 110 n. 22
Stalker, D. 47 n. 30
Stamps, D. L. 126 n. 7, 127 n. 10, 128 n. 13
Stark, R. 128 n. 12, 128 n. 14, 130, 132, 135, 140 n. 48
Stienstra, N. 117 n. 29, 117 n. 32
Stringfellow, W. 53 n. 40

Thistleton, Anthony C. 103 n. 6, 104 n. 9
Toorn, Karel van der 78 n. 31, 108 n. 14
Trapp, T. H. 106 n. 13
Trible, Phyllis 119 n. 36
Trobisch, Walter 17, 18
Tsumura, D. T. 9, 69 n. 23, 69 n. 24, 70 n. 26, 78 n. 31

Uehlinger, Christoph 107 n. 13, 109 n. 20

Vanhoozer, Kevin J. 103 n. 6
Van Leeuwen, R. 96 n. 14
Vaux, Roland de 37 n. 5
Verhey, A. 127 n. 9

Waltke, B. 96 n. 15
Watson, Francis 103 n. 6
Weems, Renita J. 101 n. 2, 117 n. 29
Wenham, Gordon J. 9, 24 n. 8, 27 n. 10
Westbrook, Raymond 111 n. 23
Westfall, Cynthia Long 9
Wiedemann, T. 161 n. 26
Wolff, H. W. 37 n. 5, 43 n. 18, 44 n. 20
Wright, Christopher J. H. 31, 59 n. 2, 61 n. 5, 64 n. 15, 68 n. 20, 102, 105 n. 10, 111 n. 23, 117 n. 32
Wright, G. Ernest 42 n. 15, 48 n. 35